THE STORY OF A YEAR: 1848

Curiosity about the past is an essential human characteristic, and the desire and the capacity to satisfy it have always been the hallmarks of great historians. The purpose of this Cassell History series is to make more readily available some significant and enduring historical works, which were widely acclaimed when they first appeared, and whose stature has only increased with the passing of time. Such books transcend the narrow limits of antiquarian scholarship and professional specialisation, and are as much a part of our general culture as great works of art or of fiction. They enliven the mind, lift the spirits and broaden our horizons, and they deserve to be brought before a new generation of readers. They are works to cherish and to delight in.

Raymond Postgate was a man of many parts, a *bon viveur* who was also a socialist, a civil servant who had been a journalist, and a historian who occasionally wrote detective novels. He was born in 1896, the son of a Cambridge Professor of Latin, and was educated at Liverpool College and St John's College, Oxford. He was a conscientious objector during the First World War, married the daughter of George Lansbury, and continued to campaign actively for socialist causes throughout the 1930s. Among his many books were *History of the British Workers* (1926); *That Devil Wilkes* (1930); *How to Make a Revolution* (1934); and, with his brother-in-law G. D. H. Cole, *The Common People, 1746–1946* (1946). Between 1951 and 1969 he was the author and editor of the *Good Food Guide*. He died in 1971.

The Story of a Year: 1848 provides a zestful and poignant account of the most tumultuous twelve months in European history between the French Revolution of 1789 and the outbreak of the First World War in 1914. It was the year of cholera and railways, of the Ten Hours Act and the California Gold Rush. But above all, it was the year when thrones tottered and trembled in France and Austria, Naples and Prussia, and when the Chartist disturbances in England seemed yet another portent of revolution. There are memorable portraits of such ardent figures as Mazzini and Garibaldi, Kossuth and Blanqui, who seemed on the brink of making a new world. But by the end of the year the forces of authority had reasserted themselves, and men like Radetzky and Louis Napoleon were firmly back in charge.

CASSELL HISTORY
Series Editor: David Cannadine

The Story of a Year: 1848

RAYMOND POSTGATE

CASSELL · LONDON

Cassell Publishers Limited
Artillery House, Artillery Row
London SW1P 1RT

© Raymond Postgate 1955

British Library Cataloguing in Publication Data

Postgate, R.W. (Raymond William), *1896-1971*
    The story of a year 1848. — *(History classics)*.
    I. Europe. Revolutions, 1848
    I. Title   II. Cassell History
    940.2'84

ISBN 0 304 32225 3

Printed and bound in Great Britain by
Biddles Ltd., Guildford and Kings Lynn

Contents

5

Acknowledgements

The line illustrations appearing on pages 70, 163, 172, 181, 190, 211, 221, 224 and 235 are reproduced by permission of *Illustrated London News*, and those on pages 11, 12, 17, 34, 51, 59, 61, 82, 93, 95, 111, 115, 119, 123, 127, 129, 159, 215, 237, 238 and 250 by courtesy of *Punch*.

Maps

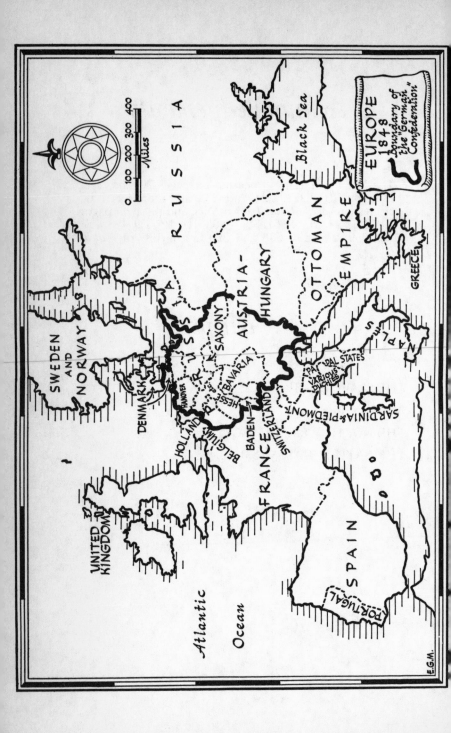

EUROPE
1848

Boundary of
the "German
Confederation"

RUSSIA

SWEDEN AND NORWAY

UNITED KINGDOM

DENMARK

PRUSSIA

HANOVER

HOLLAND

BELGIUM

HESSE

SAXONY

BAVARIA

BADEN

SWITZERLAND

AUSTRIA-HUNGARY

FRANCE

SARDINIA+PIEDMONT

PAPAL STATES

VARIOUS DUCHIES

NAPLES

OTTOMAN EMPIRE

GREECE

Black Sea

SPAIN

PORTUGAL

Atlantic Ocean

0 100 200 300 400
Miles

E.G.M.

Prefatory Note

THIS is not a book with a purpose; what reflections or arguments there are in it are only made in passing. Its intention is merely to enable a reader to live through one Victorian year, starting on January the first and ending on December 31st. It deals therefore chiefly with the events that an observer would have noticed; it tells the story, that is, and does not attempt to fill in the background except in so far as a particular event brings it in to the light. A deeper and larger study would have had to investigate wage rates, population figures, social customs, foreign and home investments and many other things, including building, furniture and clothing. These last, which formed the visible background, have been suggested by the lavish illustration the publishers have made possible; the rest will have to wait for another sort of book.

Nothing, of course, is invented here; the sources for each event will be found recorded at the end of the book. I would like to take this opportunity to thank Mr. R. H. Wilenski for guiding me in the search for Augustus Egg. Neither he, nor anyone else but I, has any responsibility for what I have written.

I

January

*

D AWN broke fine almost everywhere on the first of January, 1848 – fine but cold. There was a bright but pale blue sky in Europe and North America, and in both continents a hard and steady wind. To Europe and the British Isles it came from the North and the East, blowing from the Ural mountains in Russia with nothing to stop it across the great European

Innocent Mirth—The Slide on the Pavement.

plain until it reached the Pyrenees; it was bitter, but it was dry. For America the similar wind came down from the almost empty Canadian north; it was if anything colder, but not so dry. In every country, its effect was the same; pipes froze and the plumbing, from the most elaborate to the most primitive, ceased to work. All the streets which were not swept and dried (which is to say, nearly every street) became covered with interrupted sheets of ice, and the comic papers in every capital were filled with identical jokes and drawings about well-to-do men in tall hats falling down on ice-slides made by small boys; these jokes had been printed in the same month for many years past and would be printed for many years in the future. But the dry cold was not wholly

The Influenza.
" THIS IS REALLY VERY KIND OF YOU TO CALL. CAN I OFFER YOU ANYTHING—A BASIN OF GRUEL, OR A GLASS OF COUGH MIXTURE? DON'T SAY NO."

unpleasant; it brought the beginning of a relief to many citizens who had been suffering for the past few weeks from a disease bred by the damp, called the influenza. It was not, as it was to become in the next century, a death-dealing disease; it seems to have been little more than a very heavy cold combined with a fever. In all countries it was dealt with in the same way. If the attack was slight, the afflicted citizen sat with his feet in a bowl of hot water into which had been mixed some mustard; his trousers were rolled up and he wore a muffler and even sometimes (if cartoonists are to be trusted) his hat; his womenfolk served him hot rum and lemon, hot whisky, or other medicinal drinks. If the disease grew worse, he retired to bed, where he was covered with a pile of blankets and given similar remedies. In both cases, any fresh air was rigorously excluded.

Wise or unwise, this was the treatment for only a part of the inhabitants of any state. In the country the nobility and the farmers followed it closely; the farm labourers and peasants as nearly as they could – their cottages were close and stuffy, anyhow, and if they were little better were at least no worse than they had been for a thousand years. In the cities the well-to-do, the moderately comfortable and the steadily employed workers followed the régime precisely. But in every large town, and most of all in the greatest of all, London, there were innumerable men and women who did not follow it, because they could not. They lay shivering on dirty straw mattresses in filthy little rooms, in narrow, dark streets where the sun never could enter and the police never dared enter. They could pile no extra blankets on their beds, for they had none; they could wear no warmer clothes, for they possessed nothing but what they stood up, or lay down, in. Whisky, rum or more often gin they could get, and somehow, despite their poverty, they almost always seemed able to buy more than they could carry. It was often difficult to say, of the bodies picked up in the streets or found in hovels, whether it was cold, or influenza, or hunger, or gin that had killed them. The parish buried them, anyhow.

In every country such pathetic corpses were being indifferently collected; they were more numerous, or perhaps merely more noticeable, in England than in any other, for two reasons. The first, that in England alone a social conscience (though it was not called that yet) had been so awakened that facts and figures had been collected on a national scale and forced upon the public attention; the second, that England as the most successful industrial country was regarded (for once not wholly wrongly) as prefiguring for good or evil what would be the condition of all other countries in the future. There were probably even worse horrors to be found in the Russian capital, St. Petersburg (which was still commonly spelt with a final 'H'); but that was the feudal capital of a semi-Oriental despot. Few people knew, fewer cared, and certainly nobody counted how many serfs or ex-serfs died of starvation or cold. Vienna, another feudal city, was almost but not quite as indifferent. The Scandinavian capitals were small towns; so too were Berlin and the innumerable other German and Italian seats of independent princes. New York, Philadelphia and Boston, the only American towns – except perhaps Baltimore – of comparable importance in the eyes of an intelligent merchant in 1848, had slums as dreadful as London's, but they also had an outlet that no European city knew. Any man to whom conditions were intolerable could go west and cut himself a living from the virgin forest or prairie. His misery was temporary; if it lasted, that was due to his physical or moral feebleness. Only in Paris was the situation comparable to London's, and here too the truth was neither fully described nor regarded.

British dirt and misery had quite recently been examined in an official report[1]* which cunningly shocked the Victorians by its intentionally disgusting descriptions.

* References will be found at the end of the book.

The floors of the miners' lodging houses in Durham and Northumberland, it said, were six inches deep in dirt, mostly potato peelings. The filth flowing from the drains of the royal borough of Windsor was so strong and revolting that it killed the crops when farmers tried to use it as manure. In Glasgow, in the narrow streets called wynds, the inhabitants had no privies, and paid

H.R.H. Prince Albert's Model House for four families

their rent partly in their own excrement, which was politely called night soil. The investigators found in these garrets several women naked at midday under blankets; they could not dress because other women were out in the only clothes that there were. In Tranent the drains were open streams in the streets; the citizens fell into them on dark nights. In Lancashire dirtiness was almost a virtue; 'My sisters never wash,' said a witness with a certain pride; in Stafford only the lunatics were free of continual fevers, because (being under restraint) they were the only people who were washed and whose rooms were kept clean. The same official who had directed the commissioners' attention to the naked women in the Glasgow wynds told them something of the effect of these conditions on family life. The children, he said, were like dogs; 'they have no names, only nick-names'; he also told them details they did not care to print of the promiscuity due to men habitually sleeping with their wives and their sisters together.

There were, as a natural result, linked groups of criminals in almost every town, known to the police and at intermittent war with them. In London there was one of the worst, called the Swell Mob, a well-to-do, ostentatious and brutal group which faintly prefigured the gangs of prohibition days in America. (It was so insolent that next year it chartered a special train to Norwich to see an execution; the police seized the train and drove it back to London.)[2] But brutality was by no means a monopoly of the towns; on the first day of January the country newspapers carried the story of the death of John Wall 'a sober, industrious and inoffensive man of about 42 or 43 years of age' living in West Town, near Nailsea in Somerset. He had been preparing the pigs' food in his cottage when he heard the shattering of glass; he rose up from his stooping position and looked towards the window. Immediately a gun was discharged a second time, wounding him in the thigh and throwing him to the ground. A face looked through the window, to see if the shot had told, and then disappeared. Before he died, Wall told the local Constable the name of the man who had looked in; it was Manfield. This man, his brother, and another man called Jakeways had gone out shooting in the district, and had failed to secure any game; 'so Jakeways said, "Come, let us shoot the old fellow" and this was agreed upon'. That was all; there seemed to be no other motive.[3]

Dickens's descriptions, of Fagin's pupils or of any others, are not exaggerations; they are photographic. They, and others, were reproduced often rather

First Night in the New House.——Awful Discovery of Black Beetles.

unctuously in foreign journals, but they gave for all their truth a false picture of society. The British citizens who rose from their overheated beds in this January could (and mostly did) congratulate themselves on starting work in a world which was improving and likely to go on improving. A long depression (they probably first considered) had come to an end; the price of stocks and shares was generally rising[4] and trade was picking up in every commodity and nearly every country within the purview of the Stock Exchange. France and India were the only important exceptions. Hygiene was being

more observed in private houses. The Duke of Wellington had brought back from India the remarkable habit
of taking a bath every day; his prestige was such that an
ever larger number of citizens was following it – if not
daily, perhaps every other day, or at the least weekly.[5]
A curiously shaped tin container, with a high back,
called a hip bath, would be put out on a large white piece
of linen called a Bath Sheet. Within it would be a large
can of hot water, coloured a grained brown and often
with the words HOT WATER on it for greater clarity; a
towel would be draped across this, and beside it (though
not standing in the bath) would be another unlabelled
jug containing cold water. There would also be a cake
of soap and some smaller towels provided; locked in
with these, the master or mistress of the house would do
whatever he or she thought right.

There were two other more important advances on
which the citizen might have congratulated himself.
The one was negative; this was the first year in which
what were called the Three Bashaws of Somerset House
ceased to reign. 'Bashaws' was the Victorian (pretty
correct) way of pronouncing what were later called
Pashas, and the three men thus oddly named were three
officials who had for thirteen years been administering
a revised Poor Law, with the assistance of a relentless
civil servant named Edwin Chadwick. Their principle
had been simple: That relief in or out of the workhouse
to the destitute (through unemployment or illness) should
be administered in such a way as to be more disagreeable
than the most disagreeable way of earning a living outside. This was called the principle of deterrence, for it
was assumed that if a man was out of work it was his own
fault and he could remedy it if he chose. If the guardians

of the poor in any district failed to observe this principle, it was the duty of the Three Bashaws to force or cajole them to do so; and this they had done. As the past thirteen years had been mainly years of depression, and as the most disagreeable ways of earning a living had in consequence been very miserable indeed, the conditions of living for a pauper had often become very horrible, and they had affected a very large number of people. Disclosures had resulted which had broken the rule of the Bashaws. The disclosure which had most affected the working class (always a sentimental group) had been the forbidding of the tolling of church bells for a pauper's funeral. The cruellest had been the Andover scandal, where the paupers were employed in crushing horse-bones for glue-making, and were so underfed that they fought each other for the green and decaying meat still adhering.

Now for the Bashaws there had been substituted a Poor Law Board, which never met, and whose powers were effectively used by its President, a conscientious, quiet and kind man named Charles Buller. He was in rank a minister of the Crown and clearly marked out for a distinguished career. (Nobody knew that he would die in November.)[6] For the largest, or at least the most industrious portion of the nation, a continual threat of misery and ill-treatment was modified if not wholly withdrawn. To the rest of the world, it was made clear that the nation which had popularized and made a success of the principle of *laissez faire* had withdrawn from it in one most important particular.

That was true of the second and far more important cause of self-congratulation. This was, indeed, a change which set going similar changes all over the civilized world. It was, in the opinion of a jaundiced and youthful observer, Karl Marx, more truly a revolution than any of the events which this year claimed the name. For 1848 was the first year of the operation of the Ten Hours' Act. On the face of it, this Act seems a weak thing to have been the beginning of reforms that went all round the world. It limited the hours of labour to ten hours a day (merely to ten) for textile workers (no others) of the female sex or under age (not for men). But this limited provision, enforced by inspection as other Acts had not been, struck neatly at the centre of British industry. The mills, at this date, were the only establishments that mattered; 'cotton was king' in economic fact as well as in aphorism. Women's labour was their basis; if the women left the mills after ten hours there would be no point in keeping them open for the men only, and everyone knew this. They had had to be closed, and this year was the first in which the results were seen.

All the economists, with few and rather visionary exceptions, knew what these would be. The most respected and temperate of them was a professor of the queer name of Nassau Senior, a man of narrow culture whose *Conversations* are among the more entertaining of forgotten books. He had subjected the probable effects of the Act to a careful investigation, from which he had discovered the principle of 'the last hour'. He had proved, by an analysis from which there seemed no escape, that it was only in the last hour of the running of the mills that any profit was made. Up till then, owing to the operation of free competition, it was invariably the case that the cost of materials, overheads, allowance for depreciation, and wages equalled the price received for the product. Only thereafter, in the last hour, was anything earned to enable the mill (or coalmine, or what you please) to show a profit and so to remain in business. Therefore, if the hours of labour were forcibly and arbitrarily reduced to ten (from eleven, twelve or even more) it was obvious that industry would come to a dead stop within a brief time. Ruin would be universal.

The opening of the new year, in which this disaster was due to occur, seems to have been awaited with a curious phlegm. It was not, after all, the first time in which an overwhelming catastrophe, officially believed in by everyone, had been expected with calm. And in fact, nothing happened. A delegation of textile workers, in caps and in fustian jackets, waited on the young Queen Victoria and presented her with a gold medal in commemoration of the Ten Hours' Act;[7] this was quite contrary to protocol (queens give, they do not receive, gold medals) but was otherwise unremarkable. The only immediately observable result of the Act was, oddly enough, a marked increase of music. The Chief Constable of Manchester, the capital of Lancashire, and thus for the moment the industrial capital of the world, was naturally watching with the greatest anxiety the effects of this new Act, and the next year he told a special committee of the House of Lords (on the Sale of Beer) of the results of his observations.[8] What he noticed had been a great increase in concerts and in dancing. Until then (he did not say this, but it seems a likely deduction) those who were in work had had to toil for so long that at the end of the day they were dropping with exhaustion, caring for nothing but sleep or perhaps a drink of gin or whisky beforehand. Barred by this new Act from working beyond ten hours, the operatives had not spent their leisure in drinking; they had attended concerts, had formed clubs for singing in harmony, and had even learned to dance.

This year, fortunately, there was watching events in Britain and Europe an observer who was probably the most intelligent American of his day. Ralph Waldo Emerson is as underestimated today as he was overestimated at his death; whatever his faults as a philosopher, he was exceptionally qualified to understand and report on Europe and Britain of 1848. There is a report on him by Thomas Cooper, the working-man Chartist, who was invited to meet him at a reception at Hampstead. A 'Chartist' was the British revolutionary of the day; Cooper was prepared to be hostile, and a less intelligent man than Emerson would have been patronizing. Emerson walked home all the way to London with Cooper – a long distance through the night in those days. His conversation, Cooper noted, 'was gentle and good'. Also, he did not talk through his nose, nor did he shout at him. Margaret Fuller, whom Cooper had also been asked to meet, had done both those things.[9]

This gentle and good reporter noticed first of all, because he was an American, something that Europeans and even Englishmen were last to observe. Great Britain, in the first days of 1848, seemed to them more democratic than most other countries. Sixteen years ago its governing caste had been dexterously overturned, in a peaceful revolution. The Reform Act of 1832 had transferred control of Parliament to the middle classes; though the personnel of the Cabinet was still through habit and courtesy mostly taken from the aristocracy everyone knew who were the real masters. The working class was more turbulent than in any other country except perhaps France. The rights of the individual were more irascibly asserted, and legally protected, than anywhere else at all. The press was free, as it was nowhere else (except, of course, in the United States).

Emerson saw something quite different. 'The Marquis of Breadalbane rides out from his house a hundred miles in a straight line to the sea, on his own property. The Duke of Sutherland owns the county of Sutherland, stretching across Scotland from sea to sea', he wrote.[10] 'The Duke of Richmond has forty thousand acres at Goodwood and three hundred thousand at Gordon Castle. The Duke of Norfolk's park in Sussex is fifteen miles in circuit.' He noted that when the famous artists Julia Grisi and Mario sang at the houses of the Duke of Wellington and other grandees a cord was stretched between them and the company, in case they might accidentally mix with their betters. Even religion was caste-ridden; the most venerated man in Britain, perhaps in Europe, the Duke of Wellington, in his own sphere 'esteems a saint only as far as he can be an army chaplain', Emerson noted, and underlined this by quoting a report of the Duke's which no native commentator would have considered shocking. ('Mr. Briscoll, by his admirable conduct and good sense, got the better of Methodism, which had appeared among the soldiers, and once among the officers.')

He was, in fact, little impressed by the quality of the religion which seemed all-powerful. 'The doctrine of the Old Testament is the religion of England; the first leaf of the New Testament it does not open. It believes in a Providence that does not treat with levity the pound sterling. The English', he went on, and then with typical conscientiousness corrected himself, 'the English and Americans cant beyond all other nations'.[11]

All the same, his verdict was not unfavourable. English education was good. Going to Oxford, 'I looked over the examination papers of the year 1848 for the various scholarships and fellowships, and I believed they would prove too severe tests for the candidates for a Bachelor's degree in Yale or Harvard'. Outside

Potts' Ornamental
Gas Bracket

Winchester he was as charmed as American tourists have always been by old-world survivals; at the Church of St. Cross he demanded and received 'a piece of bread and a draught of beer which the founder Henry de Blois in 1136 commanded to be given to everyone who should ask for it at the gate'. But he also noticed that the chief use of the foundation by then was to provide an income of £2,000 ($15,000 or more by present prices) for the local clergyman. He summed up his verdict in a phrase which caused some natural resentment at home: 'RESULT. England is the best of actual nations.'[12]

If he had been less percipient than he was, and, like most of his fellow-journalists, had judged by the surface, he could have adduced further reasons for his verdict. Gastronomy: this year seemed to indicate that English cooking might again become the best in the world. The English had fed better than other nations for centuries; in the last century the superiority of their inns over foreigners' (especially the French) had been commented on by all travellers. But in the last quarter of a century doubts had been creeping in; perhaps British menus were not excellent, merely profuse? Prestige had now been restored by a master-hand (unfortunately, French). Alexis Soyer this year resumed his place as chef of the Reform Club. M. Soyer was the author of *The Gastronomic Regenerator*, a vast book of recipes and kitchen management which was making a profound change already, and is indeed a much better and more imaginative guide than Mrs. Beeton's compilation which accident has preserved alone from that era. He also wrote *The Modern Housewife*, an exchange of letters on household management between two ladies named Eloise and Hortense whose style was an imitation of the worse passages in Rousseau and was greatly praised by reviewers. He made (what is as rare in fact as it is common in boasts) some actual culinary discoveries which have lasted: *cutlets Reform* are his. As well as a great cook, he was a public benefactor. He had taken leave of absence last year to organize relief in Dublin, during the Irish Famine. His success had startled the government and silenced every critic; he had devised and operated field kitchens for mass cooking which ninety years later had not been superseded. Nine thousand meals a day had been served; this month,

unsatisfied by his dignified position at the Reform Club
(where he could be, and was, disrespectful to the most
eminent politicians), he was contemplating some smaller
relief activities in the eternally miserable East End of
London. He would hold an exhibition of the paintings
of his late and adored wife, Emma, and charge for
entrance to it. Great personages would not dare to do
anything but praise, and from the profits he would start
a soup kitchen in Spitalfields. Fat-faced, with an elegant
fuzz of whisker and huge, dark, rolling eyes, his portrait
gasconades at us still from his biography. We are not
greatly surprised that, despite his 'life-long unchanging
devotion to his sainted wife', a young woman arrived
from Paris with an eight-year-old boy whom he had to
recognize as his son; nor yet that the rigid Liberals of the
Reform Club for once decided to make no comment
whatever upon the occurrence.[13]

The newspapers were full of accounts of new inventions which were making life more civilized and delight-
ful every month. There was a patent Metallic Lava,
similar but superior to the emissions from Vesuvius,
which would shortly be used to pave the streets; it was
lighter and more durable than anything else existing.
There was Pearl Marmoratum, a paste invented by two
dentists in Berners Street, London, and marketed by
them; it was used for filling decayed teeth and became
the same colour as the tooth around it. There was
Rowlands' Odonto, a tooth powder at 2s. 9d. a box
made of 'the most *recherché*' oriental herbs. There were
coloured daguerro-type miniatures, an obviously more
exact substitute for the art of the portrait painter, which
would no longer be needed. Perhaps the most striking
of all inventions was the Idrotobolic Hat, which this

month Johnson & Co., of 118 Regent Street, made a determined effort to establish as the indispensable head-gear for the man of position in London (and therefore, in due course, of the world). Being well educated in Greek, their customers would know that the initial 'I' was long, as was the first 'o', but that the other vowels were short. It should be pronounced Eye-drohtobollic, and came, of course, from the Greek *Idros* (genitive

Chair in papier maché Manufactured by Messrs. Jennens and Bettridge of Belgrave Square

idrotos), meaning sweat, and – *bolos*, throwing away; it meant Disperser of Perspiration. In the leather band at the back of the hat was 'a grooved apparatus making a series of small channels' which assisted aeration, and in the crown of the hat (a top-hat, naturally) was a small valve, which was controllable by the wearer. No picture, unfortunately, survives of this valuable and unusual garment, but Messrs. Johnson sold a large number, including one to M. Soyer.[14]

If an observer had been required to sum up in one word what was the chief characteristic of the world he saw around him, the word would have been 'stability'.

It might, perhaps, be disputed whether progress was real, or would continue; very few people would have disputed that there was a general and well-founded feeling of security. No sudden changes were to be expected; society was well established. And this was not merely true of Britain; it was true everywhere.

It was true even in that country where rapid and profound change was most ordinary, the United States of America. The States presented to the outer world, as they have done since, two or more irreconcilable portraits of themselves, and the opinions of a critic varied according to the portrait he preferred. But for the majority of foreigners, the face that America presented was that typified by the gentle and good Emerson. The New England civilization which he typified was one in which pacifism was a practicable policy, social justice an acknowledged object, democracy a matter of course, and a rather homely and prosy culture within the reach of everyone. That is to say, it was to foreign despots and aristocrats a nuisance and a bad example, whose sole merit was that, if left alone, it kept itself to itself, or at least to its own continent. To democrats and revolutionaries it was the promised land. All that they hoped for, it had achieved. Liberty and equality were already there and, no matter what was said by bigots such as the dying Captain Marryat (whose *Diary In America* 'gave great offence' and was apologized for in his obituary), the people were as a natural result happy, prosperous and virtuous (with the exception of the Southern States, where, inexplicably, slavery still remained). Julian Harney, the most uncompromising revolutionary in England, in a few months began to publish serially in his journal[15] the full text of the Constitution of the new state of Ohio, as an example of what Englishmen and Frenchmen might achieve if they deserved it. 'Since the debased and corrupt condition of our monarchical tyrannies is responsible for our miserable condition, what might we not expect from statesmen produced under an Ohio constitution?' (The constitution he printed varied only in trifling details from the Ohio Constitution of the days of Warren Harding and Harry Daugherty.) The most unselfish

Tonkin's Ornamental Iron Bedstead exhibited three years later at the Great Exhibition

and noblest of Europeans were soon to make a vain but dramatic attempt to push the world forward; they none of them, poor or rich, doubted that America led and would continue to lead the world in tolerance, liberty and social justice. There was no question in their mind which would be the first Socialist state, or *République sociale* – the phrases were just coming into use, though their exact meaning was vague.

But even they expected no sensational events this year. The American President, J. K. Polk, was a second-rate and wordy man, by origin an obscure Democrat from

Tennessee. He owed his position to a deadlock between two much abler men, Cass and Van Buren; but even if he had been a man of far more definite character he could have done nothing. This year was a Presidential election year, and he would not be re-elected. A President in such a position is at his most insignificant. 1848, even the most naïve knew, would be for the United States a year of frenziedly violent speech and of almost complete inaction. Every politician would be manœuvring for position, and the most important part of such manœuvres is to avoid giving offence to any interest. Almost any political action will hurt someone; abuse hurts nobody. The States would be filled with the roaring noise of an engine that is not in gear.

This was the more certain in that President Polk had seen, or was about to see, the achievement of most of his fairly limited aims. He wanted to settle the recurrent squabble with Britain over the Oregon boundary, to reduce the tariff (or at least prevent its rise) and to extend the boundaries of the United States to the West. Of them all, this last had been most sensationally fulfilled by what (in another hemisphere and another age) would have been called a cynical imperialist war; a vast area, adding 40 per cent. or so to the Union, had been conquered from the weaker Republic of Mexico. The Mexicans were still delaying signing the treaty, but the outcome of the war (whose total direct cost was 48 million dollars) was undisputed. It also, in the President's rather confused opinion, proved the capacity of republican governments 'to prosecute a just and necessary foreign war'. 'The war with Great Britain in 1812,' he added uncomfortably, 'shed but little light on the subject.'[16] The greater part of the newly annexed area

was called California. It was sparsely inhabited, and
much of it was desolate and useless. (One portion this
year earned the name of Death Valley.) There was a
small and not very reputable English-speaking immigrant colony among what were still called 'the
Spaniards'; they had for a while even set up an independent 'Bear State' of California. But the new lands
could not be given a territorial government, because
that would have brought up the question of the legaliza-
tion of slavery within it; and neither Polk nor any of his
colleagues intended to raise any unpleasant problems
this year.

It was in this virgin land that there occurred this
month, unnoticed, what was to prove one of the two
most important events of the year for America's immediate future. Some forty miles south of what is now
Sacramento, a man called James W. Marshall was
building a saw-mill on the American River. On January
24th he noticed in the tail-race some glittering yellow
particles. He collected them and took them to his
partner; they made some tests and decided they were
gold. They also decided to keep their discovery strictly
secret.[17] The other event was almost equally unnoticed.
A man called John Brown, a rather brutal and fanatical
man in some ways, but a passionate hater of slavery, had
just moved to Springfield the year before. This year,
while he was nominally and very incompetently operat-
ing there a firm of wool-merchants called Perkins and
Brown, he was surveying the district for a place where he
and his sons, like the Judges of the Old Testament, would
strike down the oppressors. About this time he picked
on a townlet called Harper's Ferry as his valley of Ajalon.

The columns of the New York papers forced – but

only momentarily – upon the world's attention the appearance of a type of American, newer and different from the sages of Boston or of Concord. John Jacob Astor had been fed at the breast by wet-nurses to keep his aged digestive organs working, and tossed in a blanket to keep his viscous blood circulating. But it would not do; he was dying.[18] He left 20 million dollars, a

MESSRS. TAYLOR & SONS' IMPROVED SHIPS' FURNITURE

(A) Walnut-wood couch, forming a bed when required, stuffed with the exhibitors' patent cork fibre, to make it buoyant when placed in the water. Each part being made portable, is immediately convertible into a floating life preserver; and the whole forms a floating surface of 50 feet, or life raft, in the case of danger at sea. (B) Walnut-wood cabinet, forming a self-acting washing-stand, and containing requisites for the dressing-room and toilette. (C) Walnut-wood cabinet, as a Davenport, forming a patent portable water-closet.

fortune that not even an archduke could match; he tried, vainly, to tie it up by his will in a sort of entail so that it should go on getting more and more enormous. He was vulgar and filthy in his habits – at a lunch he once wiped his fingers on Miss Gallatin's sleeve. He made his wealth wickedly – he secured his initial fortune by buying furs from Indians with rum, which first sent the tribes mad and murderous and finally exterminated them. He used this money to buy land in New York, which he rack-rented, and through which he became the most extensive single slum-landlord in the world. He would use any lie to make a profit, and some of his lies it was impossible not to admire; for example, in 1808 he had broken a blockade of the China trade by transforming a coolie into 'Punqua Wing Chong, a Chinese mandarin' who it was imperative should be allowed to return to his own country. His last act, before dying, is reported by his biographer to have been to insist on his rent from an old woman who had 'had misfortunes'.

Electro-plate upon German silver: Wilkinson's Ornamental
Venison Dish

The agent protested, but Astor insisted; in the end Astor junior gave the agent the money and told him to pay it to his father as from the old woman. 'There,' said the dying man gleefully. 'I told you she'd pay if you went the right way to work with her.' Astor House, which he built, was 'the marvel of the age. Towering six stories into the air, it boasted three hundred rooms and seventeen bathrooms, black walnut instead of mahogany, a marvellous electrical device for signalling rooms, keys on the doors, a bowl and a pitcher in every room.'[19]

There was yet a third type of American whom the world knew and whom its cartoonists recorded. None of the 1848 Americans correspond to the typical American whom cartoonists draw today – large, round-faced, clean-shaven, bespectacled, plump, talkative, a synthesis of Senator Claghorn and Mr. Magoo. The Emersonian New Englander was tallish, bony, whiskered

LIBERTY, EQUALITY, FRATERNITY.
DEDICATED TO THE SMARTEST NATION IN ALL CREATION.

and earnest-faced, recalling in some degree the goatee-bearded Uncle Sam. Lincoln a decade later was a more rugged version of the same type. That type is not totally extinct yet, but it is rarer. But the last type, if it is not extinct, is at least never recorded. In 1848 it looks at us repeatedly from the cartoons of *Punch* and similar papers.[20] The man is thin, and dressed in a suit of white or some light-coloured material. He slouches, and his

manner is insolent. He wears a soft, light flat hat;
underneath it his forehead is low and his eyes are slits.
He is clean-shaven, except perhaps for some short,
Spanish-style sideburns. Out of his thin mouth hangs a
narrow black cigar or cheroot. His accent is drawling;
his favourite opening is a word which the journalists
represent by 'Waal'. He is a sailor, a skipper, and he
commands one of those unequalledly fast 'clippers' that
sail from Baltimore or more southerly ports. But he is
unlikely to be only concerned in bringing the tea crop
from China. He is probably also a slaver. He is most
often a Yankee, but those he serves are Southerners,
though officially they repudiate him, and have very
largely succeeded in escaping the horror and contempt
that his trade and he provoke.

Crossing the Atlantic back to Europe, the optimist of
January, 1848, could have hesitated over one country
where disorder might perhaps break out – a British isle,
the island of Ireland. Distress was indeed always there,
but just now it was wider, and was having more than
usually horrible consequences. The great potato famine
of 1846 was now over; its results had been, apparently,
firstly to split the Conservative party throughout and
enforce the repeal of the Corn Laws, and, secondly, to
cause a mass emigration of ruined peasants to the
United States, where they brought with them nothing
but their hunger and an abiding hatred of the English.
But the results of a great catastrophe are never so
limited; this had left Ireland a ruined, cruel and miserable country, where murder was an everyday occurrence.
The whole island seemed on the way to savagery, and the
collapse of decency and humanity appeared to have
affected even those who should have most resisted it.

The Vatican on the 3rd of this month found it necessary to send an almost unexampled letter of reproach to the Irish Roman Catholic bishops. It referred to the 'desecration' of the churches by their use for secular and party strife, and the 'reports which have reached us of the frequent murders' and of some of the clergy 'giving indirect provocation from the pulpit, or, at least, extenuating the guilt of these murders'. The Sacred Congregation, it said indeed, could 'not bring itself to believe such reports, so extensively noised abroad', but after that formal disclaimer it ordered each bishop to give 'satisfactory and speedy information' on how true the reports were and to compel their clergy to watch over the spiritual interests of their people only and not to 'bring the ministry into disrepute'.[21]

Houses were left empty, shops were abandoned, 'the shopkeepers flying'. Five of his relatives conspired to poison Father Macguire, perhaps the most celebrated preacher of the day. The Limerick, Ennis, Clare and Clonmel trials, this month, were such a sequence of callous murders that the chroniclers despaired of recording them adequately: William Ryan, 'one of the most ill-looking ruffians ever seen in this country', had murdered nine people; 'six ill-looking young ruffians named Michael Lorney, Jeremiah Gavin, Michael Madigan, Daniel Lorney and Patrick Gleeson, all of whom appeared to be about twenty years of age ... and politely bared their heads when recognized by witnesses', dragged young Catherine Moloney with nothing on her but a frock out into a bog; two brothers Howard, and a man named Rourke, blackened their faces and broke in on a small farmer named Hourigan; unable to find him, they shot his wife and threw her still alive on the fire; then they burst into a bedroom where a sick boy was lying, rolled him out of his bed on to the floor and killed him there. Which were the more infamous, the murderers or those who testified for the police, it was hard to say. William Dwyer, an 'approver' at Clonmel, was 'a stout, broad-shouldered fellow, about twenty-five years old, with as villainous an expression as was ever stamped on a human face'. Nicholas Garraghan said he had taken part in the plot to kill a Mr. Bailey because two of his relatives had asked him to. 'Then,' said counsel, 'I suppose you'd murder me if they'd asked you?' 'By gob, I would,' was the reply.[22]

A group of men, in all earnestness and in all innocence, identified themselves with the men in the dock at Ennis, Limerick and Clare; they believed that they had found the source of all this savagery in English misrule and that they and the Howards and Lorneys were engaged in the same struggle. The rhetoric of the Young Irelanders has thrilled their successors for a hundred years; but rarely can any revolutionaries have been in fact so far separated from the peasantry for whom they believed they were speaking. Among their ablest and most popular speaker was John Meagher; here is an extract from one of his speeches, preserved by a not unkindly historian.[23]

I am not one of those tame moralists who say that liberty is not worth one drop of blood. Against this miserable maxim the noblest virtue that has saved and sanctified humanity appears in judgment. From the blue waters of the Bay of Salamis; from the valley over which the sun stood still and lit the Israelite to victory; from the Cathedral in

which the sword of Poland has been sheathed in
the shroud of Kosciusko; from the convent of
St. Isidore where the fiery hand that rent the
ensign ~~of St.~~ George upon the plains of Ulster
has mouldered into dust; from the sands of the
desert where the wild genius of the Algerine so long
has scared the eagle of the Pyrenees; from the ducal
palace in this kingdom where the memory of the
gallant and seditious Geraldine enhances more than
royal favour the splendour of his race; from the
solitary grave within this mute city which a dying
request has left without an epitaph – O! from
every spot where heroism has had a sacrifice or a
triumph a voice breaks in upon the cringing
crowd that cherishes this maxim, crying: *Away
with it! Away with it!*

How many of the ordinary Irish, reflected the historian, how many of those convicted in January could have
understood any of this rhetoric, which its speaker and
his friends were certain was thrilling the island from
Kerry to Donegal? Not one in one hundred; and very
shortly the proof of this was to be made humiliatingly
clear. For good or evil, mostly for evil, the established
order in Ireland was – established.

The rest of Europe appeared established also, and on a
pattern different from that of today. That pattern was
not greatly changed until 1918, and is still to some extent
the background map of anyone who grew up before the
first world war. An outline of this map as it was in 1848
will be found in this book. It was based upon the
decisions of the Congress of Vienna after the defeat of
Napoleon in 1815; these in their turn largely reaffirmed

the boundaries of a previous century, accepting some destruction which the French Revolution had shown to be necessary (or at least irremediable) and restoring one iniquity – the partition of Poland – which even some conservative circles were inclined to regret. To the East lay the great undifferentiated bulk of Russia, under the autocratic Tsar. Short flashes of Western civilization had illuminated its darkness, particularly during the reign of Alexander I, but they had never reached the Russian people; the only civilized elements were to be found in a minority of the tiny minority of educated men and women, all well-born or at least well-to-do by Russian standards. Of these the more independent had now to live abroad as exiles; they impressed their companions there as hysterical, morbid, entertaining, lovable, unreliable and unimportant. Polish exiles were far more important; they at least knew their own aims, and provided in any European capital a knot of gallant and romantic men prepared to offer their swords to anyone who would challenge despotism. In Russia itself there was nothing to be seen but an uncounted and uncountable number of obedient peasants. The West was to come into contact with them in a few short years in the Crimean war; one of the survivors of the famous Light Brigade was to be asked if anything particular had impressed him as he charged; he said, yes, the solid vastness of their ranks and a light but distinct smell of musk that arose from them.

There was a profound, and well based fear, among all the educated men of Europe, that this great grey mass, smelling slightly of musk, might move west and engulf them, as it had engulfed three-quarters of Poland. Fortunately, its rulers had of recent years turned it eastwards, where it was occupying Turcoman, Chinese and Siberian Khanates and provinces of which the world knew and cared nothing. The world cared a little more for the plans of conquests in Persia and India, which the Russian government seemed even then to be slowly meditating; but these projects were on the whole distant. The régime was as rigid in the prevention of freedom of thought and as callous and shifty in its official actions as its successor a hundred years later; but it was less efficient. It cared very little for the lives of its peasants and workers; it had almost mystical care for the preservation of the régime. The cult of the little father, the Tsar, was more emotional, but less extravagant, than the adulation of Louis XIV; it was longer-lived than that of Stalin. The régime was medieval; its Tsar was a gorgeous despot consecrated by centuries of obedience, its Church was as ignorant and servile as it had been in 1348 (if not more so), the various ranks of its nobility and commoners and serfs were fixed by law and tradition, the sufferings of the ordinary man or woman and the arrogance of their superiors were unquestioned, accepted by tradition and (one might almost say) automatic and innocent. For that very reason, perhaps, the régime was regarded with the more apprehension; the writings of all those who felt its nearness – Heine, Marx, Engels, Freiligrath, Kossuth, Blanc, Harney, Urquhart – express a hatred, contempt and fear of everything Russian which would provide a rich quarry for any propagandist who wished to dig in it today.

Round to the south was the decaying Ottoman empire, which held all of what later was Rumania, Bulgaria and Albania, part of Greece, and the southern two-thirds of Yugoslavia. Its slack and corrupt authority extended vaguely over Asiatic Turkey, Mesopotamia, Syria, the cultivated parts of Arabia, and Tripoli. Its control of Egypt was even fainter. It was no danger to anyone, and continued to exist mostly because the Powers could not unite to destroy it. It offered another example of medievalism, that of the Moslem Middle Ages in decay; it served to provide romantic tourists like Benjamin Disraeli with rather facile reflections on the mystery of the East and the decay of great civilizations, and preachers everywhere with evidence of the superiority of Christianity.

The small portion of the Turkish empire which had been recently freed (by a short and quarrelsome co-operation of Britain, France and Russia) was the Peloponnese and a strip of the mainland of Greece. It was a sentimentality derived from their classical reading which had induced the English governing class to take part in that adventure. A member of the House of Lords had written:

> The mountains look on Marathon
> And Marathon looks on the sea;
> And, musing there an hour alone,
> I dreamed that Greece might yet be free.

Looking now at what they had liberated, they saw a squabbling, dirty, cruel, lying, cowardly population under a feeble and unloved German prince, and they were more inclined to echo Byron's later line, and spare:

> For Greeks a blush, for Greece a tear.

There was nothing in that miserable principality and its mendicant inhabitants to encourage, and plenty to warn against, any similar adventure in the future; the lesson had been noted in various Foreign Offices, but especially in London.

Cradled, as it were, between the two half-barbarous empires was another which was equally determinedly feudal but by no means so barbarous. Moreover, it was older established than they – indeed, older than any other in the world, including the British monarchy. It could claim a thousand years with assurance; allowed but a small latitude, it could link itself with the Roman Empire and add nearly another nine hundred. Until his defeats by Napoleon had caused him to abandon it, its ruler had kept the title of 'Emperor' from the Holy Roman Empire of the middle ages. He still held it as Austrian Emperor; he was also King of Hungary; what appertained to him was *'kaiserlich und königlich'*. *'K. und K.'* stamped on metals, carved in stone, or printed on paper had an air of perpetuity about it; it has not lost it altogether yet, and the traveller (when he can reach these lands) looks at it still with a certain melancholy respect. The most powerful man in the Austro-Hungarian empire was Prince von Metternich, who had directed its policy for forty years and was by universal consent the most able and successful foreign minister in Europe, or the world. His object had been, at home and abroad, to prevent change. Its basis was as simple as that; Metternich thereby merely rationalized and carried out the instinctive reactions of conservatives throughout the continent to the disastrous years of the French Revolution and Napoleon. No political changes (economic changes, so far as they were controllable by governments, which in Austria was very far, counted as political) should be made except by the free will of the rulers of the various states, who held their position by the will of God, not by the will of the people. The rulers themselves should on the whole be decorously discouraged by their fellow sovereigns from willing such changes; where changes were called for by the people of any country the ruler of that country should be assisted to frustrate this demand by force. This very month Metternich induced the French king to join with his own master in warning Switzerland that a commercial blockade, encircling nearly the whole Republic, would be enforced if she made any constitutional change without their joint consent.[24] He was the visible symbol for all Europe of the improbability of any change; inside the Empire he had been even more successful in preventing change than elsewhere. There was almost a Chinese wall around it: it had only one port (Trieste) through which western goods or ideas could enter. The towns were small; guilds still existed and operated; ranks were strictly observed and the lower classes knew themselves for inferiors. Alfred, Prince Windischgrätz, one of the pillars of the throne, said, 'Human beings begin at barons' (an earlier form of the phrase 'niggers begin at Calais', and not meant wholly, if at all, as a joke).[25] But with all that, Vienna was not St. Petersburg, nor Constantinople. It was the seat of a civilization; it cultivated, within its closed garden, music and the arts. There were students at the university, there and in Budapest, though their curriculum was closely scrutinized. Nor would it have been true to say there was no political liberty at all. Metternich was merely opposed to change; historians have been inaccurate in calling him a 'reactionary'. Those rights which existed in the ancient constitutions of this varied empire were preserved by him. There was a powerful Diet in

Hungary, consisting of Magnates and Deputies, and subsidiary Diets in Croatia and Transylvania. They had powers, which they exercised; the Croatian Diet, for example, in 1844 had annulled a Hungarian decision establishing religious freedom. True, only the *nobiles* elected the Hungarian Diet, but there were 550,000 of them out of an adult male population of about 4 million, so the word 'nobles' is a poor translation; and the peasants, though their rights were restricted, were not serfs as in Russia. In their county meetings, when properly summoned (over which the government was inclined to make difficulties) the *nobiles* even had the right to annul royal decrees.

But the Hungarians, like the Germans, were a privileged race. The Empire was kept in order by a simple device; its variety of races was turned from a weakness to a strength by always garrisoning one nationality with the soldiers of another. Italian regiments in Croatia, Hungarian in Italy, Czech in Austria, Austrian in Poland – such was the simple formula. It was made easier by the official belief that the Austro-Germans and Hungarians were more civilized than the others, which flattered these two nations. Of these others there were several who were at that time mostly called Wallacks, Sclaves and Italians. Wallacks, or Vlachs, have since learned to call themselves Rùmanians; they inhabited parts of Hungary. Sclaves, now called Slavs, were divided into Croats in Hungary and Czechs under Austria; the Poles of Austrian Poland (Galicia) were also recognized as Slavs, but Austrian rule was so mild compared with Russian or Prussian that the likelihood of any effective opposition from them to the règime was slight. The subdivisions that we have recently learned – Slovaks, Slovenes, Ruthenians – were at this time noted by nobody. Nor did the most enlightened opinion consider even the larger Slav units likely to survive. 'The Tschechian nationality is dying', stated Marx and Engels roundly this year;[26] the 'Slavonians', they said, as a whole merely represented barbarism, and their leaders who pretended otherwise were 'phthisical' men who should give place to Germans.[27] The characters of both Sclaves and Wallacks are summarized by a less ungenerous English observer:[28]

The Sclaves are naturally slow in comprehension and apt to be servile to their superiors but with exception of the Saxon they are the most industrious race inhabiting Hungary, though their too frequent vice of drunkenness unhappily prevents them reaping the fruits of their industry. . . . The Wallacks are in a lower state of civilization than any other race. They are said to be treacherous, revengeful and cowardly, but as they have been long subjected to oppression and ill-treatment from their superiors (whether their own countrymen or foreigners) their character is naturally deteriorated. They are besides ignorant and superstitious, all being members of the Greek Church; but have shown good qualities when treated with kindness.

No such words could be used of Italians; they were a people of ancient civilization and continually, if ineffectually, struggled against their enslavement. A large part of Italy – Venetia and Lombardy – was under direct Austrian rule, and this month a fresh and severe edict had been issued against subversive agitation there. The rest was under nominally independent Dukes and

Grand Dukes (Modena, Parma, Tuscany) who were in fact dependent on Austria, and under the King of Naples and Sicily, a man as cruel and cowardly as he was crooked. Two Italian sovereigns alone behaved in such a way as to raise the hopes of Italian patriots; Pope Pius IX and King Charles Albert of Sardinia and Piedmont had introduced reforms into their dominions.

The complicated structure of the Austrian Empire rambled into yet another country, Germany. In so far as Austria, Bohemia and Moravia were concerned (but not for the rest), it was part of what was called the German Confederation. This was a shadowy body, called into existence to replace the Holy Roman Empire. To it also belonged the King of Prussia, except for those parts of his dominions seized from Poland, and a great number of lesser potentates, mostly autocrats like him. They were, effectively, independent sovereigns, though German patriots hoped that somehow the Confederation could be strengthened until it became a real German state. They had their individual characteristics: Frederick William of Prussia was a military martinet, imitating his great ancestor, but verbose, vacillating, and sentimental; King Ludwig of Bavaria was partly mad and kept as mistress a 'glamorous Spanish dancer' calling herself Lola Montez (her real name was Lizzie Gilbert); the King of Hanover was one-eyed and possibly a murderer; the Grand Duke of Baden was gentle and cultivated. But they nearly all shared one characteristic – devotion to protocol. The least dignity was insisted upon as rigidly as the greatest; the snobbishness and silliness of these innumerable little courts had, by every observer's account, an important and deleterious effect on the German character. The smallest courts were as stiff as the greatest. Prince Henry the Seventy-Second of Reuss-Lobenstein-Ebersdorf had a standing order which can serve as an example of a score of others:

> For 20 years I have rigidly maintained one principle, viz. that everyone shall be called by his proper title. This does not always happen; I shall therefore fix a fine of 1 thaler on whoever is in My service and does not call another who is in My service by his proper title.[29]

The same prince, three years before, had had the following item inserted in his *Official Gazette*:

> His most Serene Highness has most graciously deigned, His All-Highest Self, most graciously to praise before the assembled troops those militia-men, six in number, who hastened to the fire which broke out in Tonna and gave their services with the most self sacrificing alacrity, and then with his own All-Highest hand to shake that of the oldest (on proof by birth certificate that he was so) as a mark of His All-Highest satisfaction.

But, with all this silliness, the German race was obviously one of the great races of the world. Its universities were world-famous; the only great philosophers of the nineteenth century were German; already the rest of the world inclined itself before German scholarship, regretting only the German lack of unity and political power.

The state which possessed, and had for some 300 years possessed, the most aggressive political power in the world, seemed for the present happily quiescent. France had twice, under Louis XIV and Napoleon, conquered and lost most of Europe, and the behaviour of her government was watched with as natural an anxiety as the behaviour of the German government in the next century. In 1830 a resurgence of revolutionary spirit had turned out Charles X, the last of the direct line of Bourbons; very fortunately, his place had been taken by Louis Philippe of the collateral Orleanist line. Constitutional rights were secured; there was a Chamber of Deputies and a House of Peers; industrial development was encouraged, companies floated and railways built; any warlike actions were taken outside Europe (Algeria had just been conquered, the final surrender taking place this month); the King was deliberately dull and unimpressive in his behaviour, with his green umbrella and heavy pear-like face deserving and liking the name of 'the middle-class monarch'. The régime bore a gratifying resemblance to the well-established British monarchy, and the minister on whom Louis Philippe had now for some years relied, M. Guizot, was also a Protestant, whose personal moral character was above reproach. But a careful observer could have noted a sinister difference between the British and French régimes. The British, slowly and with difficulty, was moving in a popular direction; larger numbers of the people took part in local and national elections, more liberty was accorded to the press, more care was taken of the poor, corruption grew less in public administration. The French régime had moved backward; since Lafayette had secured the acceptance of Louis Philippe by certifying him 'a Republican king', the press had been censored more and more, political associations had been proscribed, the franchise had been limited, and the Chamber of Deputies had been corrupted until it was mainly an instrument of the royal will. Some liberty still remained, no doubt; it was confined to the middle class, it had to be circumspectly used, and any opposition was ultimately powerless. There was such an Opposition, based on a handful of Deputies (pretty well all constitutional monarchists) and how harmless it was could be judged by the fact that its method of agitation was to hold banquets, at which speeches would be delivered criticizing M. Guizot. The reputation of this minister had been recently tarnished. Over the complex matter of the Spanish Succession he had lied to the Powers, promising to prevent a marriage which in due course would have united the French and Spanish thrones; but this might well have been the fault of his over-smart master. No such excuse could be offered for a scandal which had just broken; it showed that bribes had been accepted by two most important ministers named Teste and Despans-Cubieres. It had been thought (noted the British Ambassador, Lord Normanby) that M. Guizot would have prevented such things;[30] as it was, he said priggishly, a statesman who did not tell the truth and whose régime was not incorruptible would surely be punished.

The most sensational event which can be found in this quiet month occurred far away, in South Africa; it was the end of what even the cautious *Annual Register* called 'the miserable Caffre war'. The word is more commonly now spelled Kaffir, and was a general term for all the barbarous Bantu tribes who, coming down from the North, had collided first with the Dutch and then with the British settlers. The Victorian Englishman is supposed to be a man of strict respectability and orthodox behaviour; later he may have been so, but at this time he was as likely to be as exuberant as a Regency eccentric. 'Romeo' Coates, who died this year, drove about London in a large kettledrum with a brass cock on the front and the motto, 'While I live I crow'; Sir Samuel Meyrick, vexed because he could not buy Goodrich Castle on the Wye, built a castle opposite and staged javelin contests.[21] The two governors of the Cape Colony, the outgoing and the incoming, were of the same extravagant type. Sir Henry Pottinger, who had just left, was notorious for his 'cold, calculated, sneering, unsympathetic demeanour'. He lived 'in open licentiousness' although he was nearly sixty years old. 'His amours would have been scandalous in a young man.' The historian here quoted adds the interesting reflection that he would in consequence have been 'much better adapted for office in India than in South Africa'.[32] He was replaced, to the universal delight, by Sir Harry Smith, who was dashing, vain, noisy and popular (though not so popular as he imagined). Smith put a rapid end to this long-dragged-out 'seventh Kaffir war'. He brought together on January 7th at King-Williamstown an assembly of tribal leaders which reads like an extract from the Old Testament:

On this day there were assembled at King-Williamstown Sandile and Anta, sons of Gaika; Kona, son of Makoma; Fini and Oba, sons of Tyali, with Koko the regent of the clan during their minority; Umhala, son of Nallambe; Tabayi, son of Umkayi; Siwani, Siyolo and Umfundisi, sons of Dushane; Nonibe, widow of Dushane; Stokwe and Sonto, sons of Eno of the Amambala clan, Toyise, son of Gasela; Tola and Bostumane of the Imidange clan; Pato, Kama, and Kobe of the Gunukwebe clan; Jan

Tshatshu of the Tinde clan; Umtirara and Mapasa of the Temu tribe; and many others of less note.[33]

He compelled them to take an oath in eleven clauses, which summarizes very well what was his main endeavour. It bound them to obey the laws of the High Commissioner, and compel their people to do so, to

JOHN BULL'S LAST BARGAIN.—PRICE £1,100,000!

disbelieve in and stop witchcraft, to prevent the violation of women, to prevent murder and to put to death murderers, to make their people honest and peaceable and stop robbery from others, to acknowledge no chief but the Queen, to abolish wife-buying, to listen to the missionaries, and once a year to bring a fat ox to King-Williamstown.

'Some of these conditions were subversive of the whole

of Kaffir society,' observes the same historian, 'and few chiefs had any intention of keeping the oath.' But the High Commissioner shocked them into temporary obedience by some simple melodrama:

'Look at that waggon,' said Sir Harry, pointing to one at a distance which had been prepared for an explosion, 'and hear me give the word *Fire!*' The train was lit and the waggon was sent skyward in a thousand pieces. 'That is what I will do to you,' he continued, 'if you do not behave yourselves.' Taking a sheet of paper in his hand: 'Do you see this?' said he. Tearing it and throwing the pieces to the wind, 'There go the treaties,' he exclaimed. 'Do you hear? No more treaties!'

His policy, and that of his government, was carefully thought out and easy to explain. There must be if possible no extension of the British Empire; at the same time, the blacks could not be left to the Dutch, who already treated them little better than slaves. In those areas for which the British had taken responsibility what was not yet called a colour bar must be suppressed; round these areas must be supported a series of tamed native states in which (a chorus of missionaries assured him) there was already a nucleus of Christianized Kaffirs who were practically civilized. Missionaries were very powerful; Mrs. Gladys Jenkins, of Cwmamman in Glamorgan, the wife of the Reverend Thomas Jenkins, was habitually called the Queen of Pondo Land; very few people, among whom was not Sir Harry, realized how optimistic their reports were. Much more trouble was expected from the Dutch, who had furiously resented the enforcement of the no-colour-bar

principle in Natal (a Dutch settlement) in 1843. But
these people who announced the natural inferiority of
the black man were themselves no convincing advertisement of white superiority. Their language was deterior-
ating into a patois called the 'Taal' or Talk; many,
perhaps a majority, were illiterate; their 'republic' was in
a state of anarchy, being governed by meetings in which
no decisions could be reached owing to the mass of inconsequent chatter, nor, if reached, could be carried
out since no settler obeyed anything but his own wishes.
Among these ineffective and degenerating 'Boers' Sir
Harry could find but one who seemed to have authority
and competence, A. W. J. Pretorius who was proposing
to lead his colleagues in a great trek north from Natal
to some place where racial equality would not be
mentioned again. Sir Harry saw him and, as he thought,
persuaded him to drop the plan. However, as a precaution he annexed to the British Crown all the land
between the Orange and the Vaal rivers, up to the
Kathamba mountains. He thought that the Dutch
farmers would do better under his rule than under the
alleged native states, in which he was right; he also
thought that he was immensely popular with them and
that in their hearts they welcomed British rule and in that
he was equally wrong.[34]

II

February

*

GWEN RAVERAT the painter notes in her auto-biography how sexual attraction has changed in her lifetime. It has moved from masculine hair to feminine legs. In the last century a young woman would write of her intended's 'lovely, long, silky, brown beard' with the same slightly guilty thrill as a young man today observes that his well-beloved's legs are smashing in a bikini. I remember my mother telling me that in the 'eighties the daring thing at Girton was to say: 'Being kissed by a man without a moustache is like eating an egg without salt.' For us, the intelligent face of Emerson is made rather ridiculous by its full whiskers. We are wrong; that hair was part of his assets and accounted for some small part of his importance. He was a glamour-boy; not to the extent that Errol Flynn or Alan Ladd are today, but to the extent that his charming appearance lent weight to his words. This was even truer of the most popular statesman in Britain, Lord Palmerston, the Foreign Secretary. We have read of him, most of us, that he had black whiskers and drove about too fast in an over-fashionable carriage; the picture suggests to us a figure of fun. Far from it; his carriage was the equivalent of a modern sports-car or the Duke of Edinburgh's plane, and those who said his whiskers were dyed were suffering from the same bitter and hopeless jealousy that makes young women say their prettier friend wears falsies. To his insolent charm Palmerston added wit and industry; it made him almost intolerable to his opponents, to the young Queen and her husband, Prince Albert, and even to some of his colleagues.

The Prime Minister, also a Whig, was a little lively man called Lord John Russell. The title needs explanation; it is an example of an illogicality which often mystified foreign observers. Not all lords, even those active in politics, sat in the House of Lords. Some were Scotch or Irish lords, of whom only an elected percentage had seats in the Lords; some were younger brothers or other relatives of the head of the family who occupied the seat. Russell and Palmerston were in the Commons, so was the titular head (as far as it had one) of the major portion of the Tory opposition, Lord George Bentinck.

The parties, the Tories and the Whigs, were not nearly so closely disciplined as Conservatives and Socialists today, nor even as closely as Republicans and Democrats. At elections they acted more or less as two orderly armies, but in between individual M.Ps. and Lords exercised immense freedom, voting against their own leaders and even turning out and reconstructing the government at times. They had no central office, as parties have today; the informal link of London club life took its place. The Tories used the Carlton Club, once in Carlton Terrace and now in Pall Mall. A Carlton member was not required to follow Tory policy regularly – Lord Ashley, in forcing through the Ten Hours' Act, had defied his colleagues – but he would have to be generally Conservative in his ways and thought. In the smaller Conservative Club, dating from

1840, there would be less tolerance, but it was also less important. The Whigs went to Brooks's and, in increasing numbers as M. Soyer's art was appreciated, to the Reform. Joe Parkes, the Birmingham lawyer who had largely engineered the Reform Act of 1832, had been its secretary, but last year he had retired, and the new man was more of a party agent. It had been intended that the Reform Club should permeate the Whigs with radicalism; but M. Soyer's gastronomic regeneration was having a discomposing effect. The rich and paunchy were filling up the Reform Club; as a result, it was Whiggism that was permeating the Radical centre.[35]

The Reform Bill of 1832 had redistributed Parliamentary seats and reorganized the franchise, giving the vote to the middle class, but not to the working class. It had removed a great number of abuses and in particular the famous pocket boroughs – though not entirely, for the morals of the new electors were the morals of Eatanswill, and forty-two of the reorganized seats were still classifiable as pocket boroughs.[36] But the general effect of the reform was obvious: it gave ultimate power to the middle class, whose tendency was towards free trade, personal liberty and the diminution of all taxes and all governmental activity. It excluded the working class, with whose aid the reform had been secured, and the workers with natural anger had ever since been agitating for a 'Charter' which would have granted universal suffrage and so caused another shift of power. They had had no success; their one-time allies had decided that reform had gone far enough. Russell had secured the name of Finality Jack for the vigour with which he expressed this.

Meanwhile, the two parties had to court their new

masters and one of them, the Tories, was just now in a very uncomfortable position for doing so. The Whig government came to the opening of Parliament this February with the anticipation of an easy session. For the Tories were split in two. As in 1922, their leaders and their most intelligent men had gone one way, and the bulk of heavy party men another. Sir Robert Peel, their leader and by a long way their ablest man, had in 1846 repealed the Corn Laws, which taxed imported corn. The Irish famine had made this necessary – 'rotten potatoes have thrown Peel into a damned fright,' said the Duke of Wellington – but the country gentlemen who made up the bulk of the party would not forgive him; they had even voted with the Whigs to turn him out of office. And, having done so, they found themselves not merely leaderless, but without the hope of finding a leader. They were almost literally speechless; as a group they were too stupid or too inarticulate to express their policy, such as it was. (It was little more than maintaining Protection for the benefit of landlords.) Attempts had been made by 'one or two country gentlemen' to take the leadership, but they proved inadequate, and the place was held, almost by default, by Lord George Bentinck, a hunting man aged forty-seven. He had certain advantages. He was strictly upright. He had cleaned up the Turf – in particular, he had proved that Running Rain, the horse which won the Derby in 1844 was actually the four-year-old Maccabaeus, a feat which secured him the respect of everyone in the House. He was industrious, and studied the subjects which came before the House, as few of his followers were capable of doing; if his resultant speeches were long and difficult to make sense of, they were at

least speeches. Often, moreover, when the press
reporters had done their kindly work, proposals which
were by no means nonsensical were found within them.
He was not a bigot; he had voted for Roman Catholic
emancipation and this month angered his followers by
voting for the emancipation of the Jews, a project which
was indeed only prevented from becoming law by the
veto of the House of Lords. But his great virtue was his
reliability. 'Lord George was never absent from his
post,' said his obituary; 'awake or asleep, there he invariably sat, from the meeting of the House until its
rising.'[37]

A fine judge of horseflesh, an upright man of good
family, assiduous in his work, not always comprehensible
and not always awake – this was not an adequate leader
for even the dullest party. The country squires found
themselves more and more turning to, and applauding
the speeches of, a man whom at first they had disliked
and distrusted. His name was Benjamin Disraeli; he
was a Jew by birth, though not by religion; and on his
first appearance in Parliament he had revolted them.
He had been dressed 'in a bottle-green frock coat and a
waistcoat of white, of the Dick Swiveller pattern, the
front of which exhibited a network of glittering chains.
Large fancy pattern pantaloons and a black tie, above
which no shirt collar was visible, completed the out-
ward man. A countenance lividly pale, set out by a pair
of intensely black eyes, and a broad but not very high
forehead, overhung by clustering ringlets of coal-black
hair, which, combed away from the right temple, fell in
bunches of well oiled small ringlets over his left cheek.'[38]
In the last session he had toned down his dress, and
appeared in a plain dark suit; for this preposterous

person had formed an equally preposterous ambition, which was no less than to become leader of the Conservative Party. He had been a Radical. He had solicited an office under Peel, and had only failed to get it because Lord Stanley, the Colonial Secretary, said that he would leave if 'that scoundrel' came in.[39] He had spoken such frightful invective that Daniel O'Connell

THE FARMERS' WILL-O'-THE-WISP.

" ——— so I charm'd their ears,   Tooth'd briers, sharp furzes, pricking goss, and thorns,
That, calf-like, they my lowing follow'd, through   Which enter'd their frail shins. *At last I left them.*"—SHAKSPEARE.

had called him 'the heir-at-law of the blasphemous thief who died upon the Cross'. He had written worse things, in his novels – defending degenerate self-indulgence ('Let me die eating ortolans to the sound of soft music'); attacking marriage ('It destroys one's nerves to be amiable every day to the same human being'); excusing frail women ('Poor creature! that is to say, wicked woman! for we are not of those who set

59

themselves against the verdict of society or ever omit to expedite, by a gentle kick, a falling friend') and even questioning their own right to rule ('There is scarcely a less dignified entity than a patrician in a panic').[40]

But it did not matter; none of it mattered, for he and only he was able to say what they wished to hear. 'I belong to a party which can triumph no more, for we have nothing left on our side except the constituencies which we have not betrayed.' How suddenly they saw themselves noble! 'To the opinions which I have expressed in this House in favour of Protection I still adhere. They sent me to this House, and if I had relinquished them I should have relinquished my seat also.' What a shrewd blow to the deserters who had followed their treacherous leader! And of Peel himself – 'a trader on other people's intelligence; a political burglar of other men's ideas'. How true and satisfying that was! During the last year they had ceased to dislike and begun to admire this sallow young man; in this session, for the first time, they were looking to him in his black suit with expectation and trust.

It was not he, however, who provided the government with its first defeat. The government's own over-confidence caused it to make a monstrous proposal. There had just been published, by some indiscretion, a letter from the Duke of Wellington in which he proved by figures that the island was totally without effective defence against a French invasion which (because of the increase in steamships) was a possibility on almost any day of the year. 'I am bordering upon seventy-seven years passed in honour. I hope that the Almighty may protect me from being the witness of the tragedy which I cannot persuade my contemporaries to take measures to avert.' On February 18th, in consequence, Lord John Russell proposed to raise £3 million to equip a militia which would number 40,000 men that year and 120,000 in 1851; for this, income tax would have to be raised from 7*d.* to 1*s.* in the £1[41] (which is the equivalent of 5 cents in the $). The reaction of the House was what

OUR NATIONAL DEFENCES.

Small Briton. "THE FRENCH INVADE US, INDEED! AND WHAT SHOULD WE BE ABOUT ALL THE TIME?—WHY, WE SHOULD, RISE LIKE ONE MAN!"

might be expected; after a short period of appalled numbness 'almost all speakers expressed dismay and reprobation; Mr. Hume amid general approval asked if they were all mad'.[42] The Chancellor of the Exchequer, Sir Charles Wood, had to withdraw the proposal *in toto*, after a few days' wait had shown that the public outside shared the members' horror of it.

Lord George had – on February 3rd – started another subject of debate which might be expected to trap the

Government again. He proposed that the blockade of the West African coast, set up to stop the slave trade, should be abandoned. Since the competition of slave grown sugar was ruining the British West Indian planters – due, he said, to the Government's treacherous free trade policy of cancelling the protective duties – more decisive action should be taken. The Government should invade and conquer the Spanish sugar-producing island of Cuba, the chief slave-depot, and keep it as compensation for £45,000,000 of defaulted Spanish bonds. In the debate which followed, Mr. Wilson considered that the West Indian planters' plight was their own fault. They had failed to develop the resources of the islands while they had the chance. Mr. Bright considered that the sufferings of the population of Yorkshire and Lancashire should be thought of first. Mr. Hume considered that in the interests of the Colonies themselves the Colonial Office should be 'locked up'. Tempers were lost; Lord John Russell said that Lord George was using methods more suited to detecting disguised racehorses and Mr. Disraeli said that the Government had falsified Sir Alexander Burnes's despatches from Kabul some years ago – it seems irrelevant, but appears to have been a successful hit. The Tories secured some unexpected support. On the 22nd a Mr. Hutt, speaking for what would now be called 'the Left' – the group of Bright, Cobden and the other Free Trade radicals – moved for and secured the appointment of a Select Committee to consider whether the West Africa squadron should not be dissolved altogether.

This was the gravest threat yet; but it had been preceded, a week before, by one almost as grave. On February 15, the case of Buron *v.* Denman had opened in the courts. Before its importance can be understood, a few lines of explanation are needed.

When a great reform is completed, the actors in it do not receive from posterity or from history the reward which they are entitled to expect. Very few reforms are in fact completed – justice, equality and humanity are never finally achieved, and from each reform there springs the need for another, and the continuation of the agitation keeps the memory of the pioneers alive. But in the rare cases when a noble work is finally done, when, say, a great evil is destroyed never to return, the world does not retain the memory of those responsible. It completes the record, closes the book and lays it on the shelf, where its dust is never disturbed again.

Of nothing is this truer than the stamping out of the slave trade. The work was long; it was deadly (men were dying six times as fast on West African duty as in any other naval station); it served no advantage of the nation concerned and indeed was at times against its interest; it was hampered by almost inextricable difficulties; it was dramatic; and it was – if you admit that the black race is equal in value to the white – among the most important and extensive reliefs that have happened to humanity. Yet who remembers Joseph Denman? Or Captain Matson? Where are the statues to Palmerston erected by the free Parliaments of the Gold Coast and Nigeria?

Señor Buron, the plaintiff, was a Spanish slaver; Captain the Honourable Joseph Denman, the defendant, was an officer of Her Majesty's Navy, serving until recently on the West Africa station. Señor Buron was suing him for the gigantic sum of £180,000, being the presumed value of slaves which Captain Denman (then only a Commander) had liberated, a prison which he had destroyed and stores which he had allowed to be pillaged by the local chief. If he won his case, no British captain would dare free a slave again. Captain Denman had influential connections in the House of Lords; the Attorney-General and Sir Alexander Cockburn, M.P., took their seats as his counsel; the judge was Baron Parke, a most meticulous man. But counsel for the plaintiff were more than hopeful; they were elated, and had reasons for their elation. For the legal justification for Captain Denman's action was very slight.

The British attempt to stop the African slave trade had been entangled in international difficulties almost from its beginning. The nations whose citizens were most engaged in the slave trade were Spain, Portugal, France, Brazil and the United States. Denmark and Holland still kept up some old fortresses on the Guinea coast; they 'were not to be trusted' in any efforts to suppress the trade, but it does not seem they were active in it.[43] The French trade was not large, but French governments were inclined to wink at it, not on principle so much as out of their age-long dislike of the British Navy. Spain and Portugal had both signed treaties or passed laws forbidding the slave trade, but the signatures of their worthless and decrepit governments were of no value. The British Government, with a weary appreciation of realities, had for years now been paying these two states bribes to honour their promise, under the thin camouflage of 'compensation'. In 1853 it was calculated that the Spaniards had received £1,134,179 and the Portuguese £2,850,965. The Spaniards intermittently made some attempt to stop the trade; but it really mattered very little whether they did or did not. General

O'Donnell, their Governor of Cuba in 1845 and 1846, encouraged the trade as much as he could; General

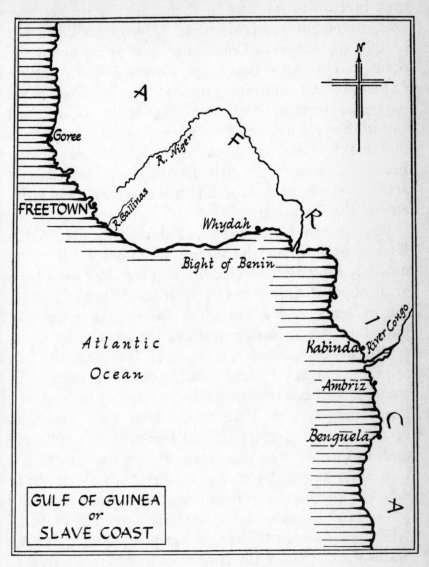

GULF OF GUINEA
or
SLAVE COAST

Valdez, his successor, discouraged it; but there were more slaves brought in under Valdez than under O'Donnell.[44] It was the speed and power of the British Navy which controlled the figures. (In 1847 the Cuban imports of slaves had been about 2,000.) The Portuguese did not even pretend to try; and in 1839 Lord Palmerston was exasperated into a typical action. 'The ships of Portugal,' he told the House of Commons, 'now prowl about the ocean, pandering to the crimes of other nations,' and an Act was passed authorizing the Navy to treat Portuguese slavers as pirates. Sixty-five slave-ships were seized within the year and the Portuguese flag was 'swept from the seas'.[45] This, much more than the famous Don Pacifico case, was 'Palmerstonian' behaviour; it was such actions which gave him his indestructible popularity among the English people.

But he could not behave Palmerstonically to the United States, though phrases in some of his Notes unwisely hinted at such longings. There had once been great hopes of American co-operation. When still under the influence of the Founding Fathers, Congress had passed an Act decreeing death as the penalty for slave-trading, and an American squadron had intermittently appeared on the Guinea coast, nominally to put the trade down. But the best is the enemy of the good; the death penalty was more severe than later American opinion would support; it was therefore not enforced, and, as there was no other penalty provided, there was in the end no penalty at all for American slavers. (Such was the explanation offered, and universally accepted; some fifteen years later, however, the signature of Abraham Lincoln to one document enforcing the Act was sufficient to kill the American trade; it vanished as instantly as the flame of a blown-out candle, without a struggle and without defenders.) The American squadron but rarely stopped a slaver; its duties were more and more to defend the freedom of the seas, which in this connection meant preventing the British from interfering with any sea-captain who chose to run up the Stars and Stripes. The American slavers enjoyed their consequent liberty, and even dramatized it. The *Martha Ann*, a fast but empty slaver, ran for many miles before a British frigate which thought it would make a capture. When caught at last after many warning shots, the Yankee captain 'broke Old Glory' from his masthead and showed that he had no slaves aboard; asked why he had not replied to signals and had made his pursuers waste two days of sailing, he answered: 'Waal, I guess we were eating our supper.' The answer was richly humorous; it was repeated in all the taverns in Havana and shouted after purple-faced British captains when they walked the streets.[46] Many Americans were disgusted by this; at least once the squadron commanders worked out a system of co-operation with the British, but it was cancelled from Washington. General Cass, who had just missed the Presidential nomination four years ago and did not intend to miss it this year, was most energetic in thwarting the British. As Ambassador in Paris, he had even succeeded in getting the French to cancel an agreement with the British, which had granted a mutual right to search ships for slaves.[47]

Great Britain had warmly and quickly recognized Brazil's independence from Portugal, and had signed with it a treaty outlawing the slave trade, only to find that no attention was paid to it. The Portuguese, wrote Palmerston in his anger, were the basest of European people 'and a Brazilian is a degenerate Portuguese'. The trade with the United States was at least nominally illegal and no one could be sure how many slaves were imported; but slaves poured in to Brazil and all society was openly based upon the trade. Though one-third of the slaves imported died, it was argued that their life in general was a happy one – they were fairly easily freed, and a freed man's son possessed all civic rights, including the right to be a deputy. They very easily became part of the family; mulattoes were very frequent, especially in priest's houses: 'you frequently go into a priest's house in the country and you are introduced to a lot of aunts and nephews and nieces or foundlings – children that are said to have been laid at their doors and left – these are the children of the priests. Of all colours.' In any case, their labour was necessary, for it was cheaper and more efficient than free labour, being 'more regular' and more easily replaced if the labourer died.[48] The trade to Cuba seemed on the decline, for good ships were needed to reach the West Indies, and the proprietors could not stand their continual losses at the hands of the Navy. But a direct trade to Brazil was springing up, for which any old vessel would do. 'They have nothing to do but set their sails and the wind blows them across the Atlantic.' Fifty thousand miserable Negroes were believed to have been carried across that way in this year.[49]

The Brazilian trade was the more difficult to kill because the Brazilians could not believe that the British really intended to stop it. Adherents of Marxist theory before it was framed, they argued that since it was against British financial interests, the Navy's repeated interference with the slavers must really be insincere. The Brazilian slave trade was in the hands of a relatively small group of Portuguese capitalists, who paid the salaries of Brazilian officials (which the government omitted to do). Fifty per cent. of their capital, or more, was raised in London. It was therefore inconceivable that the British would seriously attempt to stop this profitable and sensible arrangement; well-informed circles in Rio reacted to news of sinkings or captures with ever-resilient confidence.[50]

Apart from diplomacy and law, nature made difficult enough the task on which Denman's colleagues had been engaged, and on which they were still engaged while the court sat. The slave coast of Africa was some 3,000 miles long; it started north of the River Gambia, near Goree, an infamous place whose name has vanished and on whose site stand the wide streets of the French town of Dakar; it extended right round the great Gulf of Benin, past the mouth of the Congo and beyond the Portuguese port of Benguela in what is now Angola. Down to the roads, river mouths and harbours of this immense coast came a steady procession of shackled men and women, leaving a trail behind them which was described to the Select Committees which Mr. Hutt had, perhaps inconsiderately, called for. Major Denham, whose narrative was read to the Lord's Committee[51] and who had ridden along the trail from which the caravans started, said:

The ground around the well at Meshroo [in Fezzan] is strewed with human skeletons of the slaves who have arrived exhausted with thirst and fatigue. Round the spot are lying more than one hundred skeletons, some of them with skin still remaining attached to the bones. We bivouacked in the midst of these remains of the victims of avarice after a long day's journey of twenty-six miles in which one of our party had counted 109 of the skeletons. . . .

While I was dozing on my horse about noon near the wells of Omah, overcome by the heat of the sun, I was suddenly awoke by crashing under my feet which startled me excessively; I found that my steed had without alarm stepped upon the perfect skeletons of two human beings, cracking their brittle bones, and by one trip of his foot separating a skull from the trunk, which rolled on like a ball before him.

The survivors who reached the coast were penned in barracoons, a word that has disappeared from the

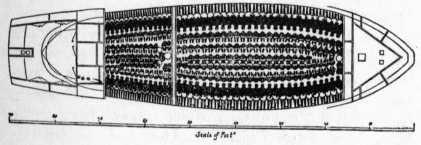

Scale of Feet

PLAN OF A SLAVE VESSEL.

English language. A barracoon was a sort of great stockade built near to the sea or river mouth; within it were long sheds made of heavy and thick piles. To these piles the slaves were chained; they were also linked to them by their necks, and the stronger slaves were beaten savagely before being attached, in order to make sure that they stayed quiet.[52] Those who survived this treatment were loaded on to a slave ship, when the time came that this could be done – for the Navy was only too frequently on the watch. Except for the Brazilian hulks, the slave-ships were splendidly constructed, the swiftest things afloat. 'Their racehorse beauty – these dashing slavers with their arrowy hulls and raking masts!'

recalled one of their captains in his old age.[53] But it
was not for their beauty only that they were the pride of
the Baltimore shipyards; they were also an admirable
example, as we should say today, of functional construction. By means of a skilled arrangement of decks and
half-decks, shown by diagrams to their lordships,[54] an
unexampled number of slaves could be packed in, lying
close together like sardines, and, when exercise and
standing up became necessary, they could be brought up
on to the top deck, and made to leap up and down in
their chains, under threat of the whip. The slave-
ships were not only distinguished by their construction;
they also had an unmistakable smell. It seems to have
been a stink compounded of sea-salt, of excrement, of
sweating and terrified bodies, and of the recently dead;
no man has smelt it in this century.

It was difficult to catch these fast boats, and the West
Africa service had its natural solemnity and terror. During the wet season, from May to October, says an old
sailing directory,[55]

> when not one solitary star is visible, nothing can
> exceed the awful grandeur and magnificence of the
> scene. The whole surface of the sea appears as one
> vast sheet of liquid fire, and the ship, sailing at the
> rate of 6 or 7 knots, causes streaks of light to be
> emitted from the sea, that throw a strong though
> sickly and appalling glare upon all the sails, creating
> an indescribable sensation in the mind which is very
> far from being agreeable, as the vessel appears to be
> surrounded by breakers on every side.

In order to catch the slavers at all, the British ships had
to cruise close inland, so as to prevent them reaching the

wide spaces of the Atlantic; when they did this their sailors died from the 'black vomit', as yellow fever was called, or from malaria. The mortality on the Home Fleet, over a period of twenty-one years, was 9·8 per 1,000; in the West Africa squadron it was 54·4.[56] The freed slaves were taken by their saviours to the new colony of Sierra Leone, where the capital had the proud name of Freetown and where they were supported at the Navy's expense for a full year. The sailors, naturally enough, celebrated the end of their mission by getting drunk ashore; the unsuspected mosquitoes killed one in two of the revellers. Sierra Leone was called the White Man's Grave; Sydney Smith said it always had two Governors, the one who was arriving and the one who was being shipped home.

The simplest way of stopping the slave trade would have been, as missionaries continually urged, to occupy the coast. But the strong anti-Imperialist sentiments which ruled Parliament forbade this; it was necessary, therefore, for the naval officers to negotiate a series of 'treaties' with the so-called native kings all along the coast. A few 'small presents' were sufficient to secure a promise to forbid the slave trade; however small they were, they must have been more valuable than the promises, whose sole use, indeed, was to appease the lawyers in London.[57]

In the evidence which was now brought before the court, it was shown that Captain Denman possessed, and had indeed signed himself, just such a treaty. It was with the King of the River Gallinas, (of whose mouth there is a picture facing page 112). He was usually called King Jack, but he was more decorously referred to in court as 'Schacka' and he 'signed' (he could not write) 'Sciacca'.

The more important signature to the treaty read 'THE
ROGERS FAMILY', a group (as so often) of white or half-
caste traders who advised the chief, and organized,
or prevented, the trade.[58] In the year 1840, it was
further proved, Denman had blockaded Gallinas River
mouth for four months on end. Not realizing the position, the Havana employers of the slavers had for all
these weeks been sending in cargoes of goods to be
bartered for slaves; Denman courteously let them pass
and they were piled up in the barracoon, whose owners
were getting desperate. They could not ship their slaves
away while Denman's ships patrolled the estuary; there
may have been, also, a disquieting gleam in the eyes of
King Jack and the Rogers family. The blockade was
hitting both the owners and the Havana traders where
it hurt – in the pocket. But Denman was no easier than
they, for his sailors were dying of the black vomit.
Fortunately, it was discovered that in King Jack's realm
and perhaps in the barracoon there was a British subject,
a black woman named Fry or Try Norman (the name is
spelt both ways) and her child. The Governor of Sierra
Leone – since Palmerston was at the Foreign Office –
instructed Denman that he should go in and rescue them.
He did so; he destroyed what called itself a fortress and
he burnt the barracoon; he freed 842 slaves and rescued
Fry Norman; he spent three days in careful and thorough
destruction, though King Jack, after a company of
British sailors had scared him thoroughly, was allowed
some handsome pickings from the Havana stores. He
saved the slavers from the revenge of their victims,
taking them coldly on board his ship. One of those
whose lives he saved was Buron, who was smirking at him
now in court.

Lord Palmerston was delighted and, knowing the value of the written word, made the Foreign Office write to the Board of Admiralty. 'I am to request,' wrote the one secretary in consequence to the other, 'that you will state to the Lords Commissioners of the Admiralty that Lord Palmerston is of the opinion that the conduct of Commander Denman . . . ought to be approved. And I am to add that Lord Palmerston would recommend that similar operations should be executed against all piratical slave trade establishments which may be met with on parts of the coast not belonging to any civilized power.' When Palmerston spoke, admirals did what they were told; the very next day this instruction was sent 'to all officers commanding Her Majesty's ships on the west coast of Africa'.[59]

Denman was promoted from Commander to Captain. The Havana slave-traders thronged round the offices of the British Consul, pathetically and ludicrously begging him to find them an honest trade.[60] Captain Matson, the next year, landed armed companies near the Congo, and led them in a long march through jungle undergrowth, under the fire of snipers hired by the slavers, to Kabinda and Ambriz, where he destroyed the 'factories' and freed 1,074 and 240 slaves respectively. Eight hundred and eighty-eight of these asked to be transported to Sierra Leone and freedom; his officers gave up their mess to the females and slept on deck; his crew went on short rations to feed the slaves.[61] It must have seemed as though the end of the trade was at hand.

Freed slaves gave their evidence in court, showing how they had been chained together through a board placed between them; Fry Norman's letters were read. Mr. Justice Parke was unmoved, for, as he and everyone

else knew, there was some more history to be related.
Lord Palmerston had lost his office in 1842 and been
replaced by Lord Aberdeen, a feeble creature whose
reputation was to be finally destroyed in the Crimean
War. Aberdeen told the Admiralty that the Government
lawyers advised that such action as Denman's was probably illegal when taken against places with which Great
Britain was not at war already. The Admiralty, which
had never shared Palmerston's enthusiasm, transmitted
these instructions at once to the sea-captains; raids
ceased; the ineffective 'blockade' was restored, and the
slave trade started up again. It was as a direct result
of this reversal that Señor Buron had brought his action;
combined with the Parliamentary attack, it was a serious
attempt to re-establish permanently the shaken slave
trade.

Such an endeavour, despite the lawyers' advice, could
never have been made if there had not been serious
political backing behind it. The backing was double.
The Tory objection to the continuation of the attempts
to suppress the trade was solid, but muddled. It was
partly an oxlike callousness to suffering, partly an
equally bovine dislike of change and trouble of any kind;
it was sustained by a belief (not wholly unjustified)
that the freed slaves in Sierra Leone usually turned out
to be 'shiftless wretches', and an honourable dismay at the
huge death roll of British sailors, in pursuance of an
object which had not been attained in a quarter of a
century and never seemed likely to be attained. Nor was
it an absolute objection; Lord George's proposed alternative of conquering Cuba was impracticable, but it was
quite seriously meant, and if it had been put to him that
in order to make it effective the British would have to

invade Brazil too, he would quite probably have advocated that also. More implacable, because it was more carefully reasoned, was the opposition from the Radicals; since they were high-principled men and intelligent, it is worth while recording the arguments by which they convinced themselves. Firstly, they said the clamour over the slave trade was a Tory device to secure compensation for West Indian sugar-planters who claimed to be suffering from slave competition after the abandonment of protection. Secondly, they said that as free labour was necessarily always more productive than slave labour the West Indies would soon be more prosperous than the others, who would be ruined. Thirdly, they said that the Navy's persecution forced the slavers to overcrowd their ships horribly and to throw the slaves into the sea when near to capture; it was therefore the Navy which was inhuman in its behaviour. Fourthly, it was clear to them that African chiefs would practice slavery, anyhow, and that life in Dahomey for a slave was worse than life in Carolina or Brazil. Finally, and most seriously, it was undeniable that recognized property rights were being destroyed by violence, and when that was allowed the basis of civilized life was being broken up.

Not all of these considerations influenced the Court; the last probably did, but more important was the legal advice cited in 1842 by Lord Aberdeen. Mr. Justice Parke was clearly of the opinion that on the basis of it Señor Buron's action should succeed, as against Captain Denman, were the Captain an ordinary defendant. But this decision was prevented by the letters and announcements of Lord Palmerston, and the interpretation which the Attorney-General placed upon them. He felt compelled to recognize (and the phrases of his judgment seemed to reflect the sort of vexation the Romans felt when Brennus the Gaul threw his sword into the scales) that the actions of Captain Denman had been ratified by the Crown, and that if Señor Buron hoped to secure compensation he must sue the Government (if he could). This action must fail.

The results of the decision were not instantly clear, but became so in a few hours. Buron or his backers would not be foolish enough to sue the Crown; the legal attack was over. The Select Committees would hear evidence upon the facts only, and these would destroy Hutt's moral case. The war on the slave trade would recommence, under happier auspices and with only Brazil as the chief antagonist.

(It may be permissible, for once, to look two years into the future. A British sloop, the *Cormorant*, is sailing along the Brazilian coast, seizing slavers as it goes. When the Brazilian forts fire on it, it turns on them and bombards them with all its six guns; the land gunners run. The Pure Brazilian Party, called on to resent this brutality, turns on the Portuguese slaving clique and chases it out; the trade is over. Lord Palmerston notes, as he thinks over his political life, that his 'greatest and purest pleasure' was that of 'forcing the Brazilians to give up their slave trade'.)[62]

The Denman trial, for all its exciting incidents, was reassuring and almost calming to the public. All was obviously well; indeed, if placidity could be made more placid, the trial would have made it so. Evil existed, but it was far away in Africa. It was being remedied by the steady and unhurried action of men of good education and breeding. They were acting in accordance with the law, which would in all cases come down ultimately on the side of virtue. Into this atmosphere of rather smug content there came, within a few hours of the end of the case, the equivalent of a violent explosion in the midst of a total silence. It was the more discomposing to thoughtful Victorians because its results suggested that where they had seen almost universal satisfaction there had in reality been almost universal dis-satisfaction. The world that they knew, so stable and so reasonable, was destroyed around them in a matter of weeks – not by invasion, civil war, or vast natural disaster, but easily and petulantly by those who lived within it, as if it had for long been a nuisance of which everyone wished to get rid.

The trouble started, as might have been expected, in Paris. Here the respectable and patient critics of King Louis Philippe and his minister Guizot were continuing their campaign of holding banquets and making speeches. Their speeches had been more bitter recently – partly because they were soured by their helplessness, partly because conditions in Paris had over the winter become extremely miserable. France had been the one country which had not recovered from the industrial depression; one man in four had been out of work, and people had been dying in the streets from hunger or cold. The Government had done nothing about it – not, indeed, that its critics were very sure what it should have done. Anyway, the Opposition announced that a banquet would be held on February 22nd at which the failure of the Guizot Cabinet would be very thoroughly exposed. The Government in reply declared that the banquet would be forbidden; angered at this new step towards autocracy, the Opposition said that it would be held, anyway. The Government collected some troops; it intended to fight. The Opposition – some deputies and some journalists – held an anxious and unhappy meeting, and then voted by eighty to seventeen to abandon the banquet. They wanted to avoid bloodshed, and, anyway, they were dispirited. The King and M. Guizot were delighted; they had scored another point of the kind they loved; they had inflicted a small defeat on their opponents at no cost to themselves. His critics had always said Louis Philippe had the soul of a shopkeeper.[63]

Both they and the official opposition, however, suffered from the commonest blindness of the well-to-do; they knew nothing of the facts of life. They imagined that three out of four Frenchmen who thought about political matters at all loved or respected or trusted them; the other quarter, maybe, hated them. The Opposition thought the same, but transposed the figures. Neither suspected that to three out of four Frenchmen who thought about them at all Louis Philippe and his ministers were third-rate, vulgar incompetents, whom they tolerated through custom and indolence, but would be glad to see the back of. The prospect of the Opposition defying this shabby crowd had interested the Parisians, and when the 22nd came, not hearing or not believing the news that the banquet had been called off, they roamed the streets and scuffled aimlessly and scatteredly with a police force called the Municipal Guard. The King thought it was nothing, but it seemed wise to call out the National Guard for the next day.

It was not wise. The Guard was a citizen body, and when it mustered next day it discovered, almost to its own surprise, that it was sick of this Government, and of the King's policy of filching, bit by bit over the years, personal and political liberties and the guarantees of honest government. It cheered for 'Reform' and declined to put down the 'agitators' who were roaming the streets. Nor were the regular soldiers much better behaved; even while marching through the streets they talked to the Parisian housewives, who put cheese and fruit in their haversacks and took out the cartridges. The King was scared, and decided to dismiss M. Guizot and send for M. Molé, also a Conservative, but better-mannered and broader-minded. The change was announced as loudly as possible and the Guard was placated. The King was short-changing it as usual, for he had arranged with Molé that there should be no reforms, but it didn't know that.

But in the evening of this day, the 23rd, a strange thing happened on the Boulevard des Capucines, near to the Foreign Office. There was a troop of soldiers there, and a procession of cheerful demonstrators tried to push by them. What exactly happened is not sure; one can only say with certainty what did not happen. A *beau jeune homme du peuple* was not deliberately slain, as the journalist Louis Blanc said. Nor was the affair deliberately provoked by a cunning revolutionary called Charles Lagrange firing a pistol at a major. At least it is clear that the troops did fire on the crowd and thirty-five or more people lay dead or dying in the road. Then suddenly the whole scene was empty. The demonstrators ran in terror; the soldiers, appalled at what they had done, seem to have run in the other direction. After a while both returned – a few of the people to pick up their dead, an officer sent to apologize. A demonstrator hit him on the nose when he tried to speak, and he went away again.[64]

The corpses were carried round Paris, and what had been contempt turned to fury. Next morning the city was full of armed and angry men, and the King was as fit to cope with it as a grocer would be to control a riot. He vacillated – first appointing a tough general from Algeria to attack the rebels, and then selecting left-wing politicians as ministers with instructions to make every concession. After a few hours he decided to abdicate. He looked round him for his successor. His eldest son, the Duke of Orleans, was dead, but there was the Duchess with her little son, the Count of Paris. He had promised the Regency, if ever there was one, to his second son, the Duke of Nemours, but Nemours was unpopular. So it had best go to the Duchess. 'Does Helen really get the Regency?' said Nemours, his lips trembling. His papa nodded, and began arrangements to drive away with his retinue to St. Cloud, in three cabs and from the back door of the palace.

The Duchess was fairly young and fairly pretty; she imagined, as royal ladies so often must, that she was far more attractive than she was. She had formed a brave and pathetic plan. She would go with her child to the Chamber of Deputies and stand on the steps of the tribune; the spectacle of royalty in distress and a lovely young mother clasping her child would appeal to the chivalry of all the deputies and the dynasty would be saved. So she did, the disappointed Nemours gallantly trailing after her. But the Chamber was in an uproar, with undesirable persons surging round it. She could scarcely get attention, and when she did, her supporters spoke so lengthily and so floridly that the moment (if there ever had been one) was lost. At last Lamartine, a poet who had always been half a Republican, told her

gently that they all sympathized with her, but that the
people of France were taking over their own destiny,
that this meant a Republic and she had better go. She
was escorted out quietly, and in a few moments 'the mob'
broke in and most of the deputies ran away. At the
Luxembourg the House of Peers, mistaking a message,
had set out two golden chairs for her and her son;

PUT OUT!

but she never came, and they too adjourned in mystifica-
tion, never to meet again.[65]

Louis Philippe drove on to Havre, where he called on
the British Consul for aid; he had decided to escape to
England. The Consul was glad enough to help him; but
he made things more difficult by adopting the guise of
the 'Consul's uncle, an English sea-captain named
Smith', and waddling round shouting, 'Where is Mrs.

Smith? Where is my old woman?' and other phrases which he felt were impenetrably idiomatic. At last they got him and his retinue on to a boat. Queen Victoria and Prince Albert gave them a house at Charlemont when he arrived in England; but they found something wrong with the pipes there; there was too much lead in the water and it gave the exiled court colic. So they had to move to the Star and Garter Inn at Richmond, and with that he and his dynasty passed out of history.[66]

When the deputies ran from the Chamber, some of the republicans or half-republicans stayed behind, and the crowd began to shout for a provisional government. Names were read out and hissed or applauded; there was inextricable confusion, and in the end the poet Lamartine led a group of those who seemed – nobody knew quite how – to be the government at the head of a procession to the Hôtel de Ville, where it was traditional for revolutionary governments to be proclaimed. They struggled slowly through crowds which were cheering, shouting and shooting (but mostly in the air) to find the Hôtel occupied by the people, exercising its right of camping in any official building or wandering up and down. They had scarcely sat down in one distant and empty room that had been found for them when a new government arrived. There had been a meeting at the offices of the *Reform*, a left-wing newspaper, which had also chosen a government, and here it was, headed by the journalist Louis Blanc. It was an embarrassing moment, saved by the quick wit of Garnier Pagés, a member of the first group, who had appointed himself Mayor of Paris. 'These gentlemen,' he said, pointing to the four newcomers, 'are the Secretaries of the Government.' They accepted this; in about an hour the distinction was forgotten and everyone was equal.

The chief defect of the Government, so chosen, was that it had no leader. Its nominal head was an old member of the Convention of the First Republic, M. Dupont, who because there were so many Duponts carried the parenthesis '(de l'Eure)' wherever he went. He was upright (as indeed were all the Government; they were men of unblemished probity), but he was very old. His signature on the first decrees quavers like that of a man who cannot hold his pen. His colleagues went their separate ways, and they mostly did not know which way to go. They have each of them been subjected to minute study by historians, and their tendencies and social milieu analysed. Their names, for the record, were Lamartine, Cremieux, Arago (the astronomer), Ledru-Rollin, Garnier-Pagés, Marie, Marrast, Blanc, Flocon and Albert (a gas-worker – probably the first working man ever to be a Cabinet Minister). But the differences between them were far less important than these studies suggest. They had two things in common. They were republicans in theory who were totally unprepared for their success. They knew that poverty, starvation and unemployment stalked through France and must be remedied, but of how to control economic processes they had no more idea than an American business-man of 1929. They fell back on symbolic decrees. They decreed the Right to Work. They announced the establishment of National Workshops. They summoned an assembly of the workers at the old House of Peers (the Luxembourg) to produce a plan for the Organization of Labour. They also abolished the death penalty.[67]

Their supporters were delighted: the 'days of February' remained for years in all men's memories as days of harmony and hope. Men and women of all classes embraced each other in the streets and assured each other that everything would be better now. Baron de Rothschild danced with a worker round a newly-planted Tree of Liberty and nobody even smiled. When a spokesman of the Paris proletariat said 'the people put three months of poverty at the disposal of the Republic', he was speaking quite seriously, and the Government equally seriously promised to abolish misery in that period. Their most hostile critic, Lord Normanby, the British Ambassador, condemned them not because their plans were impracticable, but because they might prove practicable. They were criminal folly, because they would upset all established society, and they were being encouraged by the very people who should have prevented them. The worst of all were the railway companies, who betrayed civilization and undermined society by agreeing to decrease working hours and even to allow their workers to share in profits. He apologized for holding any communications with such a 'terrorist' Government; it was necessary, for no other ambassador had the authority necessary to impress such bandits, and 'many large [English] families were wandering about the plain of St. Denis' trying to find the broken-down railway.[68] The investors of the City of London agreed with him; the fall in the prices of every kind of stock was catastrophic.[69]

III

March

*

THE disapproval of the London investors seemed to be shared by nobody else. Almost all over Europe the people greeted the French news with the equivalent of the banal sentence: 'What a good idea!' They did not, indeed, decide to chase out their reigning monarchs and replace them by republics. Few kings were as widely despised as Louis Philippe, and the word 'republic' was still an alarming one, suggesting proscription, terror and possibly war. They would prefer their kings, whom they generally saw distortedly through the pink glass of tradition, to turn into almost powerless constitutional monarchs like Victoria of England or Leopold of Belgium – benign friends offering good advice to free citizens. They did not yet know that hardly any of the monarchs was benign, and none of them was both able and willing to offer good advice. They thought most of securing reforms that seemed more important – trial by jury, personal freedom, freedom of the press, the election of a democratic Parliament which should have the only right to make laws, the dismissal of the old ministers, their replacement by democrats, and the abolition of all noble and royal privileges. Within a few hours of the arrival of the Paris newspapers it seemed obvious to them that all these things could be achieved, and that without much difficulty.

Others than they saw this. The King of the Netherlands, the slimmest Dutchman of them all, announced the granting of nearly all these concessions before there was time to organise anybody to ask for them. In the Grand Duchy of Baden, after a noisy meeting at Mannheim, there was a rather ridiculous race to Carlsruhe where the old Diet was sitting, between Herr Doktor Mathy the moderate liberal who wanted it to vote all these reforms, and Herr Doktor Hecker the extremist who wanted to dissolve it by violence before it could agree to them. Mathy won by a few hours. A determined procession was actually marching through the streets of Copenhagen in Denmark to teach the new King Frederick his place, when he met it eagerly; by an almost incredible coincidence, he explained, he had been privately working on a most advanced project for some while, and here in his hand was the decree for a totally democratic constitution. Simplicity or good manners prevented any Dane saying that the coincidence was not almost, but quite, incredible. The inhabitants of Hesse were ruder: they told the Elector 'the people mistrusts your Royal Highness personally . . . and sees a lack of straightforwardness'. They got approximately the same constitution. The most interesting events, to a German public which was as snobbishly romantic as the readers of an English tabloid, occurred in Bavaria. King Ludwig, who wrote poetry, held concerts and paid sculptors and painters to decorate his palaces, had just sent away his concubine, Lola Montez, and installed a pious and Conservative ministry. Lola had been regarded as democratic, and on the rather limited grounds that she was pretty, swore like a carter, sometimes wore trousers, and had a bulldog whom she had trained (she said) to bite Jesuits only. The King had not finally given her up; he said she had silly ideas and perhaps was bewitched; she must stay at what we should now call a clinic in a town called Weinsberg, under the care of a Dr. Kerner, who knew all about 'magnetism and spiritual possession'. The doctor fed her on raspberry juice and one small white cake a day; she got much thinner (trousers had not really suited her very well recently) and was by now quite ready to come back and behave herself. Munich, like every other German capital, was in an uproar; the citizens were exercising their new-found freedom in writing poems, in singing songs disrespectful to the King, firing guns into the air and dressing up (as Germans everywhere were doing) in gaily coloured jackets, red and black trousers and hats with large feathers. But they did not call for the return of Lola. They did call for the removal of the ministers, whom King Ludwig disliked anyway, and they cheered him when he appeared at the Opera with the Queen instead of the woman they called 'The Public Mistress'. After a hysterical fortnight, however, Ludwig decided to abdicate; he instructed the papers to publish the full text of a final poem by himself (on the subject of Ingratitude, addressed to the Bavarian people), and presented to them his son, Maximilian II, certified to be a constitutionalist. Lola decided to go to England.

But it was all very well to be entertained by these theatricalities, or to reduce Henry LXXII of Reuss-Lobenstein-Ebersdorf to tears. The real centres of power lay elsewhere, as the King of Saxony indicated when his Board of Censors tried to resign (on grounds which no censors would be manly enough to announce today – that their job was in its nature dishonourable). So long

as King Frederick William of Prussia controlled the best
and most powerful and successful army in the world, and
Prince von Metternich (on behalf of an Emperor named
Ferdinand) the most ancient Empire in the world, any
uproars in minor courts were mere passing noise. A
group of Rhineland professors and doctors had actually
met at Heidelberg to arrange for a 'Fore-Parliament' to
meet in Frankfort as a precursor to a real Parliament of
a united democratic Germany; they were all chicken
counting.[70]

Within a day or two the chickens had hatched. On
March 13th Prince von Metternich was in flight; on
March 19th King Frederick William's ever-victorious
army was evacuating Berlin. The Fore-Parliament
actually met on the last day of the month.

The explosion in both Austria and Prussia was un-
speakably surprising; the Prussian's defeat was the more
complete. What the King's intention had been is
uncertain: behind the façade of a Prussian martinet there
was a vain, garrulous, sentimental and boastful man, not
very intelligent, not truthful, not brave. It is probably
useless to try to deduce a consistent policy from the
behaviour of a man so neurotic; but it is possible that the
outcry for a united Germany had suggested to him that
he might gain for himself an All-German crown while
keeping his power at home intact. Certainly, while
writing hysterical letters to Queen Victoria about the
horrible news from France, he had made verbal concessions pretending to welcome the new spirit in Germany
– enough to excite the Berliners without giving them any
solid advantages. On March 18th he announced in
vague terms that there would be freedom of the press;
there followed (as in Paris) demonstrations partly of

satisfaction and partly of unsatisfaction; then (again as in Paris) soldiers shot down demonstrators for some unexplained reason and barricades and fighting resulted. There was more severe fighting in the evening; artillery was used; and during the night the frightened King issued a proclamation 'To My Dear Berliners!' asking them to pull down the barricades, after which the soldiers would be confined to barracks. 'Your loving Queen and sincerely true Mother and Friend, who lies prostrate with pain and grief, joins with mine her heartfelt and tearful supplications.'[71] To his surprise, the placard only annoyed his loyal subjects; they fought more obstinately. The Prince of Prussia, Prince William, was quite sure what should be done; more soldiers should be brought in and civilians should be shot down steadily until the honour of the Army was restored. But the King was more scrupulous or more frightened; he sent the troops away and granted all the reforms which were asked. The rebel dead were carried in a long procession past the palace while he stood on the balcony, handkerchief to his nose, weeping as freely as any crocodile. The Prince of Prussia left hastily for England, losing his last aura of romance as he shaved off his fine, smooth beard. There was a Liberal ministry in the Chancellery, there was quiet in the squares, and stuck in a pump in the Breitestrasse was an unexploded shell, on which had been pasted the words, TO MY DEAR BERLINERS.

The revolt in the Austrian Empire was less destructive, but astonished the world more. French papers had been read aloud to crowds in the Vienna cafés ever since the first day of the month, but it was not there that the revolution started. It was at Pressburg, at a meeting of the Hungarian Diet on March 3rd, that a handsome, histrionic young lawyer named Kossuth delivered a speech declaring that 'a pestilential wind blows towards us from the charnel house of the Vienna system' and demanding a free constitution. The Viennese were not going to be outdone by a people whom they had always regarded as romantic but backward cavalrymen; on the 12th the students of the University waited on the Emperor Ferdinand, a middle-aged epileptic, with a petition for universal suffrage, arming of the people, a free press and personal liberties. They received a vague answer, and retired. Now, in Vienna (as in many other cities) there were no 'organised masses of workers', nor of employers either. Nothing fitted into the revolutionary classifications which later Marxist theory has made almost compulsory. There was a closely knit, rich and supremely confident group of landed aristocrats. There was a large, variegated group of traders and professional men of all kinds, with no cohesion at all. There were some hundreds of students, all young, most much above the rest of the population in intelligence, and linked in a solidarity even closer than the aristocrats. There was, in the suburbs particularly, a large working class – working in small factories, or for themselves, or with one or two employees, who looked to the students for instruction, themselves providing most of the physical strength. They rioted when advised to, and when the violence seemed to be getting out of hand, a company of students in their academic uniform would race to the battle, call the workers back – and be obeyed. In between, the students would enter the working-class districts and hold discussions on a free press, religious freedom, trial by jury, and so forth. On the 13th this curious alliance went into action. There was some vigorous street-fighting for which the aristocrats were quite unprepared. Archdukes Albert and Maximilian tried to fight the rebels, Archduke John tried to mediate, the Emperor had a fit, Prince Windischgrätz asked to be made a dictator so as to shoot down the students and workers. Before long resistance began to collapse; the Emperor granted free speech and the arming of the people in the National Guard; most significant of all, Metternich was dismissed and fled. His exit was not very dignified: he took refuge in the same doctor's establishment at Weinsberg where Lola Montez had been, and made his host run up a red flag on the house. He sat in a room in the tower practising the 'Marseillaise' on a fiddle, until he decided that he too had better escape to England. When he got to Rotterdam he found that the boat that had left before his had carried Lola. 'I thank Heaven for preserving me from such a contact', he wrote, and so he too vanishes from history.[72]

The collapse of the 'Vienna system' meant the collapse of the old régime everywhere. In forty-eight hours Kossuth and his fellow Hungarian M.Ps. received their constitution and took it back to Budapest. Hungarians were free. (As for 'Sclaves and Wallacks', they were not mentioned.) In five days – on March 18th – the largest town in Austrian Italy, Milan, rose and after five more days beat the Austrian army out of the town. This was something new: in other cities the people had rioted and defied soldiers of their own race, who were unprepared and had not been too willing to fight, any-how. But the Austrian army thus fairly beaten had no sympathy with the revolt, was excellently equipped, had been prepared for trouble for some months, and was commanded by Marshal Radetzky, who was able (as his next campaign was to show), energetic (he was a weekly fornicator at the age of eighty-one) and merciless (he massacred with cold calm a few months later). If a people commonly assumed to be degenerate could chase him and his army away, the old world had indeed ended.[73]   In Venice, too, a solemn little lawyer with ulcers, named Daniel Manin, left his house, dressed in a shining top hat and black coat, with a white sash across

THE DELECTABLE BALLAD OF THE FOUR KINGS OF ITALY:
SHOWING HOW THEY EACH TOOK HIS ROUGH DRAUGHT OF A CONSTITUTION, AND HOW IT SORE MISLIKED SOME OF THEM.

The Pope. "I FEEL ALL THE BETTER FOR MY DOSE, AND I THINK YOUR MAJESTIES CANNOT DO BETTER THAN FOLLOW MY EXAMPLE."
King of Naples. "TAKE AWAY THAT NASTY COMPOUND."
King of Sardinia. "AS NAPLES IS TAKING IT, I MAY AS WELL."
King of Denmark. "I SUPPOSE THERE IS NO HELP FOR IT, SO HERE GOES!"
King of Prussia. "I MIXED MINE MYSELF, AND SO I KNOW IT'S ALL RIGHT."

it and a sword strapped on that he did not know how to use; he put himself at the head of about 200 'civic guards', and with the aid of the dock-workers outwitted rather than out-fought the Austrian governor and garrison; in three days the old 'Republic of St. Mark' was re-established, with a democratic constitution instead of Doges.   The Patriarch of Venice blessed the flag with the winged lion of St. Mark on it, and, in order to meet any political possibilities, also the red, white and green tricolour, the French tricolour and the American stars and stripes.[74]

93

The rest of Italy had not waited for the Austrians to collapse (though the Italian revolutions would have been put down at once if they had not). Charles Albert, the King of Sardinia and Piedmont had promulgated the usual constitution – for once, honestly meaning it and keeping his word later even under difficulties. So too had the Dukes and Grand Dukes of Parma, Modena and Tuscany. The King of Naples and Sicily had done the same, being prodded thereto by a Sicilian revolt even before France moved. To a public sated with wonders, none of this brought surprise; its eyes were on the centre of Italy, on that band of territory called the States of the Church and under the direct rule of the Pope. In the past, so far from being an example to Christendom, this had been a disgrace even in a peninsula tolerant of squalidness, corruption, poverty, illiteracy and cruelty. Personal freedom did not exist. 'Tied up by ropes to the walls of filthy prisons, or to the galleys of Civitavecchia, or more mercifully executed by gibbeting or shooting in the back, the Pope's enemies perished and were forgotten.'[75] Eighteen months ago Gregory XVI had died; his successor, a gentle priest taking the title of Pius IX, had recalled some exiles, released some prisoners, and given partial freedom of speech. The wave of gratitude that resulted had embarrassed him, for of political ideas he had practically none. Now his people were pointedly waiting for something more; he announced the creation of an elected assembly to assist the cardinals in governing the Papal States, and gave half the portfolios in his Cabinet to laymen. The concession was not great, but it was enough to delight his people, and to set some of them dreaming of a united, democratic Italy of which the Pope would be head. Not everyone

found this an agreeable dream, especially not King
Charles Albert of Piedmont, who already saw no
objections to himself as the ruler of Italy.

There was little to record elsewhere on the Continent,
except the promise of the usual constitution in Sweden
-and-Norway. Spain was occupied in a dreary civil

A TRIP TO PARIS IN SEARCH OF LIBERTY.

war about dynastic claims, and the peoples of the
Russian and Turkish empires were too benighted to
know or care what happened. France, the fountain and
origin of the revolutions, was now in a state of doubt
and confusion which was, perhaps, an inevitable sequel
to the first days of beatific enthusiasms. Just as every
War Office is fully prepared to win the last war, so all
revolutionaries are prepared to carry through the last
revolution. Lenin and Trotsky studied the history of

the Paris Commune carefully, avoiding its errors and arranging to repeat its successes. Robespierre drew lessons from the life of Cromwell. Robert Emmet learned from the mistakes of '98; Pearse and Connolly from those of Robert Emmet. So the new French government was determined to repeat the victories and avoid the mistakes of 1789 and 1792; in the middle of a wholly modern industrial crisis the Ministers were anguishedly trying to read the moral of the conflicts between Jacobins and Girondins. Dupont (de l'Eure) lived wholly in the past. Lamartine, as Foreign Minister, felt himself a Girondin who had seen the mistake of the Gironde. It was, in brief, to have gone to war; in an eloquent message of instructions to every French ambassador, he said that France's sympathy with freedom everywhere would everywhere stop short at the use of armed force.[76] It was a useful action; it calmed the enemies of the revolution, especially those across the Channel. He used, like Kerensky, this same long-flowing eloquence to soothe and charm the deputations which came one after another to demand work and food, or something less reasonable like the invasion of Poland; but each time he had more difficulty in getting them to retire. For the Treasury was bankrupt, and there was really neither work nor food to offer the citizens. The least helpless Minister was the one who was considered most impractical, dapper little Louis Blanc, the Socialist journalist. At the head of his Commission of Workers at the Luxembourg (the first Soviet in history, as social students have noticed) he was outlining a programme which was as empirical as Roosevelt's 'New Deal' and in some odd ways recalls it. As a self-appointed arbiter, the Commission negotiated agreements in various trades for shorter hours and stabilized wages, hoping thereby to diminish unemployment (as was later to be the hope of America's N.I.R.A.); it put much more trust in its integrated plan for reopening as co-operative productive societies the businesses and factories which were closing down, the credit being supplied by the State which would allot to the bankrupt owners bonds giving them a claim on a proportion of the establishments' profits. (It might be compared, if the comparison is worth carrying on, to Roosevelt's W.P.A.) A National Assembly, elected by universal suffrage, was to be chosen at the end of April, and Blanc recognized that this scheme would have to be submitted to it for approval; but the atmosphere was still so cordial that he believed the approval would be forthcoming. However, while he and his Commission were completing their plans, another Minister, M. Marie, was in charge of the National Workshops which had already been instituted by Government decree, and what was going on in them if it is to be compared to anything must be compared to the Republican view of the New Deal. There was chaos, noise and waste; and practically no work was done. M. Marie's economic ideas were rather like those of Lord Normanby – that road-mending, soldiering and digging were pretty well the only sort of work the State should ever offer the unemployed – and though he had an earnest administrator named Thomas under him the experiment was bound to be an expensive failure from the first.[77] The chief of police was a huge man with a very small head named Marc Caussidière; his deductions from the first French Revolution were that sincere Republicans should carry arms (which led to there being three other police forces besides his own) but that there should be no terror. He therefore spared some police spies whom he found even in the ranks of his own friends; one of them, De la Hodde, has left a dramatic account of how he was exposed. He stood defying Caussidière and his colleagues, he says, leaning on his elbow against a marble mantelpiece in the Prefecture, and his noble demeanour caused them to abandon their plans to murder him; we can believe him if we choose, but his book is that of a lout and a liar and there are other, very different accounts.[78]

Since the great revolution had been inspired and controlled by clubs like the Jacobins, Feuillants, and Cordeliers, there were bound to be clubs in 1848; and so there were, half a hundred of them. Some of them have a considerable importance in the history of social and political ideas – Cabet's utopianism and Proudhon's anarchism are to be found in every text book, and L. A. Blanqui was the first formulator of what was afterwards called the 'dictatorship of the proletariat'. His speeches were inflexible and terrifying; he frightened the Parisians more than anyone had done since Hebert in 1794. His very appearance was appalling.

'The memory of him', [wrote de Tocqueville] 'has always filled me with horror and disgust. His face was wan and emaciated, his lips were white, he had a sickly pallor and the appearance of a mouldy corpse; he wore no linen that I could see; an old frock-coat tightly covered his thin withered limbs; he looked as if he had passed his life in a sewer and had just left it.'

He was a vivid contrast to the Minister of the Interior, who had also studied the French Revolution, and believed he could be Danton, but a successful Danton. Ledru-Rollin was big, round-faced, pink, and voluble. He liked good food and wine almost as well as the sound of his excellent speeches. The success of the Jacobins, he decided, had been due to their sending out deputies 'on mission' into the provinces to make sure that the lead of Paris was followed. He would send out agents to do the same. His chief adviser in this was Amandine Lucile Aurore Dudevant, a voluminous writer (109 volumes) of some genius and a woman for whose life 'irregular' is a most inadequate word. She is better known as George Sand. The instructions which she drafted for his agents for the purpose of 'making' the elections said:[79]

> Eighteen years of falsehood oppose obstacles to the system of truth, which human breath cannot dispel. The elections, if they do not inaugurate the triumph of social truth, if they are but an expression of the interests of a class, extorted from the confiding loyalty of the people – the elections, which ought to be the redemption of the Republic, will be its ruin; there can be no doubt of that. Only one resource will in that case be left to the people, who erected the barricades; and that will be, to manifest its will a second time, and to adjourn the decision of a false national representation.

Madame Aurore did not realize, though Ledru Rollin should have done, that it is better not to publish the intention of dissolving a Parliament one dislikes if one wishes to win the election. At that, the Minister of the Interior was wiser than most of his colleagues; he at least understood that provincial opinion was important. But neither he nor any other townsman knew what provincial opinion was likely to be. Provincial opinion was peasant opinion; and it was a long time since the French peasant had been consulted. He was different from his successor of today in two ways. He was poor and discontented, and in politics he knew only one name; that was the name of the man who had died twenty-seven years ago in St. Helena.

It would not be true to say that the series of European revolutions had had no effect in Britain. It had produced very great excitement; *The Times*, as Emerson noted with surprise, printed on March 1st the largest number ever issued by a daily paper – 54,000.[80] The Chartists, the working-class revolutionaries, summoned a Convention for April 4th which was to imitate, somehow, the Continental successes. There was a serious riot in Glasgow on the 6th, at which what are called seditious cries were heard, but on investigation it appeared that common thieves had intelligently adopted republican slogans for the purpose of looting the shops of fifty-thousand pounds' worth of goods. On the same day a meeting was called in Trafalgar Square to protest once again against the monstrous proposal to increase the income tax; the organizer abandoned it, but it was taken up by a young journalist named George Reynolds, who moved Chartist resolutions and encouraged the demonstrators to fight the police, with some success. But here too the ease with which the audience turned aside to pillage shops seemed to show they were less earnest-minded than they should have been. The truth was that the excitement was partly factitious, or at least was merely the excitement of spectators. After sixteen years of defeats, the Chartist movement was breaking up: its leaders were having a hard job to whip up their followers' enthusiasms enough for them to take advantage of the revolutionary opportunity. They did their best; the flag of the English Republic (bars of red, green and white) was flown at meetings; decisions to arm and drill were announced; Feargus O'Connor their leader, a big noisy Irishman, with an oddly empty face, addressed his followers in weekly letters as 'Imperial Chartists!'[81]

How far they would succeed was still uncertain; meanwhile, the most interesting event of the month only indirectly linked up with the revolutionary excitement. It was a wrestle between the free press and the Church; the Right Reverend the Lord Bishop of Exeter brought into court on a charge of libel one Thomas Latimer, a resolute Liberal editor of that town.[82] The affairs of the Church of England attracted far more passionate interest then than today, partly because there was more piety, but more because of its great power. There had already been this year attempts, amounting nearly to brawling in church, to prevent the enthronement of the Bishops of Hereford and Manchester. The feeling against Phillpotts, the prosecuting Bishop, was far stronger. Sydney Smith, usually a gentle man, wrote: 'I must believe in the Apostolic Succession; there is no other way to account for the descent of the Bishop of Exeter from Judas Iscariot.' Henry Phillpotts was a small man with (writes the biographer of Latimer) 'a face at the same time interesting and terrible, with hair already becoming thin, an intellectual, rather bulging forehead, restless twinkling eyes, a proud, curving nose, and a rat-trap mouth whose corners dropped in line with a crescent of deep wrinkles extending from his nostrils to his chin'.[83] He had arrived at his eminence by political sycophancy, changing with the government of the day.

He had used his influence and power (which in those days was great) for the benefit of his eighteen children; the list of ecclesiastical posts and sinecures he had secured for them made scandalous reading even in the 1840s. His sense of duty was small; when the cholera struck Exeter in 1832 and his spiritual help was needed, he merely ran away. He was merciless to his inferiors in suppressing any deviation in doctrine or even any personal friendliness towards a Methodist or other heretic; in those days, it should be remembered, for a clergyman to be deprived of his living on such grounds was often to be deprived of his living in exact fact. Ecclesiastical politics have always been tortuous, and the devices by which Phillpotts got office after office and benefice after benefice into his own gift are difficult to follow today, but they had been exposed one by one and year after year by Thomas Latimer in his *Western Times*, where the details can still be found. Little, indeed, can be said for Phillpotts except that he seems to have genuinely thought that he incarnated the Church, that attacks on him were therefore to be suppressed as mercilessly as evil doctrine should be, and that in increasing his power and wealth he was in some way acting for the greater glory of God. He had once secured a criminal conviction of a journalist named Williams for attacking the clergy (he had himself described Williams as 'a miserable mercenary who eats the bread of prostitution', but a bishop need not fear being sued for libel); he had for long planned to catch Latimer too. It was in a protest against one of many pieces of small persecution that he decided Latimer had overreached himself. There was a poor curate called John Shore whom the Bishop had jockeyed out of his living because of some personal vindictiveness. This living was the curacy of Bridgetown Chapel, a new building built and maintained by the elderly Duke of Somerset. The Duke, discovering that the Bishop's action was legal, though dishonourable, and pitying the curate, who was in poverty and misery, took back the chapel, re-registered it as a free church, and appointed Mr. Shore to it. The Bishop in answer sent for Mr. Shore and proved to him that by the then-existing law he could never officiate in a dissenting chapel, having once taken Anglican orders; therefore, he was in a position where the Bishop would prevent him earning a living within the Church and the law would prevent him earning one outside it. The man was thus satisfactorily ruined; his persecutor went up to London and in the House of Lords made a statement that the Duke had 'violated his engagements'. This was a gross affront, even from a bishop; the Duke's son, Lord Seymour, at a speech at Totnes, said it was 'an unqualified falsehood'. But Latimer thought this too mild; he reviewed Phillpotts's career, character and manners in a special leader in the *Western Times*. It was for this that Phillpotts was suing him for criminal libel. The leader was, indeed, a piece of writing whose meaning could not possibly be misunderstood. The Bishop, it said, was 'everlastingly in hot water, but never clean'. 'He is so notorious a brawler, that any story respecting his rule and discipline, provided it does not contain the imputation of any of the milder virtues, is received without question.' In the debate on the Shore case,

his reply is so directly the opposite of the truth, that he stands branded as a consecrated, careless perverter of facts, and one who does no credit to the mitre which he is paid £200 a week or thereabouts to wear. . . . We started with the idea of drawing a contrast between His Grace of Somerset and the old gentleman in question – (indeed, he is always an old gentleman in question, for no one ever takes for granted all he says) – but we shall not pursue it, because the statement of the names contains the whole parallel.'

Any reader of Trollope would have recognized the scene when the Bishop drove into Exeter. The Palace, which he rarely visited, was opened and warmed, and a banquet ordered to celebrate his victory. Mr. Justice Platt, his friend, took the case; the Bishop and some of his family sat on his left in the magistrates' box. (Latimer sat in an ordinary seat in the well of the court.) The Bishop had secured a 'special' jury — that is, a jury exclusively of the well-to-do – and his lawyers challenged the jurors ingeniously, so that at the end the jury consisted of eleven Conservatives and one Liberal. Latimer's article was re-read, with expressions of horror, by the Bishop's counsel. All the correspondence over Shore's curacy, and the building and withdrawal of the chapel by the Duke, was read and commented on at tedious length. The first living witness was the Bishop himself. Sir Alexander Cockburn, for Latimer, cross-examined him politely, but firmly. He made him admit that he had altered the *Hansard* proof of his attack on the Duke so as to make it ruder. He elicited evidence of personal spite in his treatment of Shore. He then went on to question him upon his general political behaviour, and on the often sordid and sometimes violent disputes in which he had been engaged. But the judge was the Bishop's friend; he refused to allow such questions to be put. Cockburn protested that the alleged libel concerned the whole of the Bishop's political life; but Baron Platt was master in his own court, and maintained his refusal. Latimer's case seemed ruined; the only question would be the length of the sentence.

Cockburn, however, was a great lawyer, in the court as well as in the study. He turned the Judge's biassed ruling into a triumph for himself. He announced that he had intended to call as witness Lord Seymour, who was in court, and to put in the Duke of Somerset's evidence taken on commission. But since the Bishop was not to be cross-examined, then neither would he call his evidence; he would proceed immediately to address the jury. This he did, with his usual incomparable skill. The dissection of the behaviour of the Bishop in the Shore case was in itself severe enough, but the jury felt (and were encouraged to feel) that behind it were even worse things which they had been prevented from hearing. 'I ask you, as twelve honourable men, whether you can believe one single word of the Bishop's statement,' he cried, and not even Mr. Justice Platt dared interrupt him. However, as soon as he had sat down, the Judge set out to destroy the effect of his speech. He re-read Latimer's article to the jurors. 'Certainly, you cannot conceive that a more base charge can possibly be made – to call a bishop a consecrated, careless perverter of facts!' He is described as speaking with 'great warmth of manner' and 'energetically'.

'Now, gentlemen, that is the libel. It directly imputes to the Bishop falsehood. It directly imputes to him that he is a wrong-minded person, that he is a *brawler* – that he is notorious as a brawler, a careless perverter of facts, no credit to the mitre which he wears. Now, gentlemen, it is for you to say whether that publication is not a defamatory libel of the Bishop.'

The jury retired, being expected to stay out only a few minutes; the Bishop had already gone back to the Palace. But they were absent a long time. Gradually the faces of the Bishop's secretaries and lawyers became whiter and more anxious. When at last the jurors reappeared, one glance at their faces showed the anxiety was justified. Their verdict was for Mr. Latimer. There was a roar of cheering which the Judge could not put down; the Bishop left Exeter in a cab without eating his banquet; all was over.

It was a victory for free speech, no doubt; but there were many foreign observers who were surprised at the attention it was receiving. When all the world was in chaos, when the foundations of Government were being torn down in almost every civilized state, was this a time to debate the defeat of a Bishop in a small provincial town in the West of England? Surely things would soon happen to shake the British out of their smug and isolated calm.

IV

April

*

IT seems, in retrospect, as if the world was indeed waiting in the month of April for England to move. Everywhere else the revolution either marked time or, if it advanced, the advance was for the first time marred or at least shadowed by some adventitious circumstance which made its supporters uneasy. In Paris there was no change; that is, there was the same sequence of noisy but not violent demonstrations, the same spate of advanced or socialistic proposals, the same failure of the National Workshops, and the same general concentration on the election for the National Assembly. In Prussia the imprisoned Polish patriots had been freed from their Berlin prison and sent off with cheers to Posen; once there, they had not made trouble for the Russians, but had massacred a number of Jews and started what looked very like an ungrateful attempt to chase the Germans out of 'the German share' of old Poland. In Germany as a whole, the Fore-Parliament had had a great success, one which nobody could deny or minimize. An All-German Parliament was being elected, and elected on a democratic basis. It would meet, and not one of the rulers of the separate states would dare to stop it. Indeed, they all pretended to desire it fervently. They were lying, it is true; King Frederick William of Prussia was writing privately:

Liberalism is a disease, just like a disease of the spine. The symptoms of the latter are (1) that the strongly convex and prominent muscle of the thumb and forefinger becomes concave by pressure, (2) that an aperient constipates, (3) that an astringent medicine purges and, at a later stage, (4) that the legs can be raised without one's being able to walk. In this way Liberalism works on the soul. . . . Black is called white, darkness light, and the victims who succumb to a sinful, God-cursed frenzy are almost, or entirely, deified. For the spirit in them – these convicts, galley slaves, sodomites etc. – is supposed to have struggled courageously upward to the sky![84]

But these opinions remained private; the German democrats continued to believe in royal and ducal loyalty, and at any rate power was still obviously in their hands. A new state was coming into being, as a result of some six weeks of speech-making and – all told – very little bloodshed. Yet even this splendid achievement was damaged by a piece of silliness. Dr. Hecker of Baden, who had been thwarted of his *coup d'état*, was the first of a type of revolutionary which was to become more and more common; he thought that to be more Left was always to be more right. In the interval between the adjournment of the Fore-Parliament and the meeting of a new Parliament, that is on April 12th, he proclaimed a German republic and marched northwards from Constance at the head of a small army. This army had largely been recruited in France by a poet named Herwegh and his wife; he was autocratic and she was practical. She was 'about 25 years of age, not pretty but agreeable, with a good figure, of middle height, with pale auburn hair and light blue or grey eyes'. She had decided to march with her husband to victory, putting on male clothes, and a considerable part of the committee-men's time had been spent in discussing whether she should cut off her hair or tuck it in under a specially made hat.[85] Hecker's other chief lieutenant was a vegetarian named Struve. The army was met by Baden and Hesse troops on the 20th, and after a short fight was defeated and broken up. All the leaders escaped, including plump young Frau Herwegh, who was wearing tight black cloth trousers, a black velvet blouse, and a broad brimmed black hat; and therefore (it is somewhat surprisingly said) looked like a schoolboy. Nothing could have been more deplorable than this escapade. Militarily, its conduct, uniforms and strategy had made German democrats laughable. Politically, it had never had any chance of success. All it had done was to make a number of influential and serious-minded democrats decide that, after all, it was obviously necessary to restore to the police and the armies some of the power that had been taken from them.

The Hungarians were enjoying their new constitution in a honeymoon of romantic loyalty, and enacting reforms which were far from being too advanced. Among these was one for the universal use of the Magyar language officially. This was, to their great surprise, resented by their 'Sclave' fellow citizens, the Croats; the Hungarians' double reply was, firstly, that Croat councillors and deputies could speak Latin if they chose and, secondly, that if they continued to make a claim for their obsolescent language the Wallacks would do the same, and have to be allowed it. This, as they expected the Slavs to see, was absurd.

In Italy, too, there had been what appeared to be a great success, clouded almost at once. King Charles Albert of Piedmont had come to the aid of the rebels of Milan 'as brother to brother and friend to friend', with what was the only disciplined and well-equipped Italian army in the world; he had inflicted a severe defeat on Radetzky's disorganized armies at the battle of Goito. This seemed to make Italian victory certain, for the moment at least. But it was already clear that Charles Albert expected to be paid for his help; and this payment would be the annexation of Lombardy and probably also Venice. The Pope had announced in an Encyclical that he would not fight against the Austrians, nor would he conceivably become the head of a federation of free Italian states. By this declaration he had turned away from liberty and democracy, and though few Italians suspected how fast and far he would go, all of them realized that there was now no hope from Rome. The republicans in Northern Italy, among whom now were both Mazzini and Garibaldi, realized furiously that a 'voluntary' request for annexation to Piedmont would have to come from Lombardy and Venice; they would be able to delay it a few weeks, and that would be all.

What happened in Britain, then, was going to be crucial, and every Continental revolutionary could predict it. (Ledru-Rollin even knew the date.) It would come in two parts, co-ordinated. There would be the national revolt of Young Ireland against the British, and the social revolt of the Chartists against the exploiters. The first proceeded, initially at least, according to plan. The British Government as was expected introduced a repressive Bill, making the speaking of treason a felony. William Smith O'Brien, the leading Irish M.P., made on April 10th a fierce speech opposing it, declaring that it forfeited and annulled the loyalty of any Irishman to the throne; he walked out of the House of Commons never to return. His young supporters in

NOT SO *VERY* UNREASONABLE!!! EH?

John. "My Mistress says she hopes you won't call a Meeting of her Creditors; but if you will leave your Bill in the usual way, it shall be properly attended to."

Ireland were already calling him too much Smith and too little O'Brien; he was going back there to prove them wrong. He was gentle, highborn and civilized, and the last man to lead a guerrilla war; but he saw no reason, nor did his followers, why he should not do in Dublin or Cork what Manin had done in Venice. It would be, however, a month or so before he could arrange this.

Meanwhile, the British revolution was proceeding faster – faster indeed than the revolutionaries altogether liked. A good number of the Chartists thought that the preparations for armed revolt were silly, and that the loud announcements of them were even sillier. Thomas Cooper was among those who withdrew and started to form small Chartist Leagues whose sole weapon should be peaceful argument. The famous 'six points' of the Charter were only these: votes for every man, equal-sized constituencies, no property qualifications for M.Ps., the ballot, annual Parliament and payment of members. In a reasonable world, argument should certainly have been able to secure most of these. But many years of propaganda had not secured them, and most Chartists thought that a sharp stroke now, while opportunity served, was the only way. Their eyes were on France: 'We'll respect the law, if the law-makers respect us; if they don't – France is a Republic!' said Ernest Jones, their most intelligent leader.[86] They seemed almost to think they *were* in France; their delegate meeting which met on April 4th was called 'The Convention', as if the year had been 1792 and the city Paris. Julian Harney, their most ferocious speaker, called himself the Friend of the People and by a careful, open-shirted disarray made himself look as much like Marat as he could without raising ridicule. There were forty-six delegates, from towns scattered rather haphazardly about the island, mostly elected by large public meetings. Nearly all of them were convinced that they both could and should be the instruments of a revolution similar to those of the Continent; their speeches showed anger and determination, though on the methods to be used they were vague or contradictory.

> Mr. Wilkinson reported that his constituents were opposed to physical force. Mr. Matthew Stevenson said there was no use in preaching patience to the starving masses. He described his constituents as being in a most wretched and horrifying condition. Mr. Ernest Jones said his constituents wished to conduct the movement, if possible, on moral force principles, but if necessary they were ready to fight to a man. They were ready to rush down from the hills of Yorkshire in aid of their brother patriots of London. Mr. James Hitchin described the people of Wigan as suffering a great amount of oppression and misery. They were ready to try one more petition but if that were rejected they would 'go to work' let the consequences be what they might.[87]

There were many more speeches to the same effect, made more repetitive and frequent by bad chairmanship. They had, at the least, the effect of whipping up the enthusiasm both of the delegates and the crowds which thronged the galleries, and of spreading alarm outside. The lowest estimate of the real Chartist strength in London is 10,000 men, partly armed, and far fewer than that had been sufficient to overturn the governments of some fifteen monarchs elsewhere during the previous six weeks. There was very good reason for fear among those who heard or read the delegates' speeches. But there was a weakness behind these fiery addresses, beyond this uncertainty over immediate methods. They were asking either too much or too little.

Too little, in the sense that their essential demands could be reduced to a very small compass. Of the six points of the Charter, only three were really important – the ballot, equal electoral districts, and universal suffrage, and these again could at need have been cut down to the last one only. The Chartists were not calling for a wholesale political and legal reconstruction such as had been secured elsewhere. There was no need to demand trial by jury; it had existed for centuries and all that could be asked was that the selection of jurors should be made more democratic. It was unnecessary to call for a free press – it already existed and those who read the obscene publications issued in the area which is now Aldwych might have even wished for a little more restriction. All that was desirable was the reduction or abolition of the press tax. There was no clamour against imprisonment without the sanction of law, or for protection against personal violences by officials or noblemen; these had ceased to be allowed for many years. There was no need to demand the transfer of real power from the Queen and the aristocracy to a popular Chamber. The effective superiority of the House of Commons over the Crown had been asserted 200 years ago and over the House of Lords sixteen years ago. There was no need to protect a man's right to his tools, his plot of land, or whatever small property he might have; they had been safeguarded for as long as anyone could remember. Indeed, the fact that all these rights were secure made many potential Chartists, especially of the middle class, languid in their support of the one demand that remained. But the delegates' support of that demand was also too much, in that it carried with it a claim which they were unable to phrase exactly but which meant an upheaval much more serious than dethroning a Queen.

Mr. Kidd said that in Oldham they entertained the idea that constant starvation was worse than death. Mr. Donovan said that 10,000 of the people of Manchester were out of work. They wished to attain the Charter without physical force, but they

Magistrate. "Now Sir, what do you want?"
Nervous Gent. "I beg your pardon, Sir; but I wish to be sworn in as a Ch—Ch'—Chartist. I mean as—a—Sp—-Sr—Special C—Constable."

wished for the Charter at all risks. Mr. Mirfield hoped that if the petition to enact the Charter were rejected they would take into their hands the government of the country and divide the land into small farms and give every man an opportunity of earning his living. (*Tremendous cheering.*)

Such speeches, unaccompanied by any practical programme such as is offered by a modern Socialist party, sounded like a threat to take either their money or their land, or both, from those who had any; it seemed that the passing of the Charter would mean that 10,000 men in Manchester alone would have to be maintained by the rest indefinitely; it would quarter hundreds of thousands of unemployed on their more fortunate fellow citizens; it would mean dividing up all farms and estates which were of a size to be run profitably – it would mean anything, in short, which a scared man could imagine, nor was there any word of reassurance in the speeches in the Convention.

Indeed, whether as a bluff or because they believed it, members of the Convention acted as though it was only a matter of time before they took over power. Feargus O'Connor, who had succeeded in making himself their unquestioned leader, said at the third meeting that he spoke of course 'as a quasi-Minister'. George Reynolds, who had chaired the recent meeting in Trafalgar Square, had the mortification of having his credentials challenged by a tall, soft-spoken mulatto named Cuffay. Wasn't he a very recent convert? Had he given evidence that he was fit to belong to a body that would have such great power? Reynolds, a fat-faced, balding young man with metal-rimmed glasses, poured out a flood of hurt protest which Cuffay accepted – going so far indeed as to join with him in a resolution demanding concrete preparations for an armed rising if the Petition to the Commons which was in hand was rejected. (Reynolds was not wholly pleased with this, and kept away from Cuffay afterwards.) O'Connor next said that the House of Commons was now of far less importance than the Convention; he would have now, however, to go to that House where he was the only Chartist M.P. If it was of no importance, then why go there? objected an old Chartist named Bronterre O'Brien, and was booed for it. Because, said O'Connor, there had been talk of forbidding the meeting and procession which was to present the Petition next Monday, April 10th, and he was going to tell the House of Commons that he would be in the front ranks of those presenting it, even if his enemies shot him dead. There was wild cheering, renewed when he announced that the Petition had 5,700,000 signatures.

The Government had in fact decided to prevent both the meeting and the procession. It was seriously alarmed, even if not so frightened as private individuals were; but it had committed itself by a proclamation, and no doubt felt that it would be far more dangerous to withdraw than to stand to its decision. One thing was in its favour: the meeting was to meet on Kennington Common, which is nowhere near Kensington, but is on the south side of the Thames. It would only be necessary to hold the river bridges firmly to prevent the Chartist forces ever reaching Westminster. That an attempt at revolution was really to be made seemed beyond doubt. Certainly O'Connor had said: 'What will happen on Monday? I can tell you. Peace and order will prevail', but he had also printed in his paper, the *Northern Star*:

If I had trafficked in your confidence I might perhaps be induced to cry – *wait, wait, wait!* But your destitution and misery and my own feeling . . . would not allow me to utter the delusive words, and therefore it is I tell you that in my soul I believe the propitious hour has arrived when our long suffering and martyrdom may be crowned with the laurels of victory.

Lord Campbell, the Chancellor of the Duchy of Lancaster, writing to his brother on the Sunday night, said: 'This may be the last time I write to you before the Republic is established! I have no serious fears of revolution, but there may be bloodshed.' The wife of a Cabinet Minister – which one is not stated, but she acted with her husband's sanction – wrote to Harriet Martineau asking her to try to bring 'the working classes to reason', fearing that 'the Chartists were about to hold the metropolis'.[88] Prince Albert, who had less charm but more sense than most of those around him, wrote to the Premier:

> Several hundred workmen have been discharged at Westminster Palace; at Buckingham Palace much fewer hands are employed than are really needed; the formation of Battersea Park has been suspended; etc., etc. Surely this is not the moment for the taxpayers to economize upon the working classes! And though I don't wish our Government to follow Louis Blanc in his system of *organization du travail*, I think the Government is bound to do what it can to help the working classes over the present moment of distress.[89]

There was no time now, anyway, to produce a conservative edition of Louis Blanc's programme; the threat was upon them and the Government called upon the greatest soldier of the century to avert it. The Duke of Wellington was put in charge of the defence of London. He brought the Horse Guards (the 'Blues') from Windsor, the 12th Lancers from Hounslow, the Grenadier Guards, the Coldstreams, and the 17th Foot from Colchester, Windsor and Dover, and the 62nd and 63rd

Foot from Winchester and Chatham. These he posted by Monday morning throughout the City and the West End, but kept them almost wholly in concealment, for, wisely and humanely, he hoped that the police and special constables would be able to handle the rebellion. Special constables were being enrolled in great numbers:

LAYING DOWN THE LAW.

Special Constable. "Now mind, you know—if I kill you, it's nothing; but if you kill me, by Jingo it's Murder."

The Times afterwards gave the figure as 170,000, and though all numbers are suspect at this time, it was probably somewhere near right. One of them was Prince Louis Napoleon Bonaparte, Napoleon's nephew and heir. He was allotted a beat in the West End which he shared with the Head Cook of the Athenaeum, who entertained him with morose comments on another French exile, Alexis Soyer, his rival at the Reform. The

specials had large white bands on their sleeves as uniforms and were armed with big staves. They were more
numerous than formidable.

> The efficiency [wrote an expert on physical culture]
> of the 200,000 special constables would have been
> doubled had each individual been inured to violent
> exercise. On that day I saw many forms cast by
> Nature in an athletic mould but wasted and bloated
> by luxury or inaction. There was no doubt
> abundance of courage, but there was also a lack of
> physical strength, of ability to strike a blow or
> robustness to endure one. . . . Many a valorous
> constable would have been captured by his own
> prisoner.[90]

A delegation from the Convention called on the
deputy chief of police, promising that the meeting
should be completely unarmed. He felt now that he
could treat them with cold rudeness, telling them to obey
the proclamation; and did so.

All Government offices were closed and barricaded,
and their staffs instructed to garrison them. Palmerston
himself took command at the Foreign Office, saw that
the windows were blocked with bound volumes of *The
Times* and armed the clerks with cutlasses and elderly
blunderbuss-like muskets called Brown Besses.[91] The
Morning Chronicle, almost certainly by Palmerston's
desire, printed a leader 'of caution and remonstrance'
to the Chartists, begging them at this last moment to
give up their plan.

> 'A large body' [it warned them] 'of cavalry and
> infantry, supported by batteries of artillery, are
> ready to act at a moment's warning. . . . A complete

line of military communication is established from the Tower to Buckingham Palace, and the whole is under the direct control of the Duke of Wellington himself. All the public offices are well garrisoned'.

Its reporters scurried round on the morning to find what the defences were like. They estimated the regular troops, so far as they could see them, at 9,000. The General Post Office was very heavily barricaded, and its staff had been given 2,000 'stand of arms', mostly, however, ancient stuff taken from the Tower of London. The Bank of England was heavily sandbagged. There was a guard of 200 on the Royal Exchange. All the shops and larger houses in the City and Westminster were closed tight and barricaded; so were they in Oxford Street and Tottenham Court Road, but the shops in Regent Street and Piccadilly had kept open with a rather conscious defiance – the latter encouraged by the fact that the Church and churchyard of St. James were wholly filled by waiting special constables. The morning was cold, dull and cloudy.

The Chartists assembled from half-past nine onwards at two main points south of the river (Elephant and Castle, and Northfields in Peckham) and at several north of the river – Clerkenwell Green, Whitechapel, Stepney Green, Finsbury Square, Russell Square and Holborn, where they were headed by the 'Robert Emmet Brigade', a disciplined body marching well enough to secure involuntary words of praise from the police. Westminster Bridge was guarded, but Blackfriars and London Bridges were open and the contingents marched steadily over them, orderly and with banners waving. The estimates of their numbers varied from 15,000 to

150,000; an opinion prepared later by 'military men' for the Government gave 23,000 on Kennington Common and near to it 'some seven or ten thousand more'. So far as is known they were unarmed. Not all were convinced Chartists; there were many who were merely discontented. Two young artists who were revolted by the Philistinism of the Royal Academy joined the procession in Russell Square and marched over Blackfriars Bridge. Their names were John Millais and Holman Hunt, but for some reason when they reached the Common they 'did not go on the grass'.[92] The most attentively watched contingent was the last of all to arrive; it was headed by a car drawn by six horses and occupied by all the members of the Convention, behind which came another drawn by four horses and carrying the vast bulk of the Petition. There followed a cortège of some 1,700 persons carrying banners, including one 'of a most singular character' bearing nothing but the words AND GUIZOT LAUGHED IMMODERATELY.[93]

Feargus O'Connor, their gross, red-haired leader, was sitting in the front of the first car with the thin, passionate, humourless lawyer Ernest Jones next to him; his thoughts must have been uncomfortable. By a mixture of bullying and promising, brought to a finer art in later years by other Irish politicians in Tammany, he had made himself an absolute boss; he had taught all the Chartists to trust him and him alone, and to do whatever he said. Now he had to face the obverse of that success; if this Monday was a failure, he and he alone would be blamed. And it is not sure that he even had a plan.

As soon as he arrived, a messenger came to him, to say that Mr. Richard Mayne, the Commissioner of

Police, was in the Horns Tavern on the edge of the
Common and wished to see him urgently. He left the
platform at once and pushed his way with some difficulty
through the crowd; when he returned, he looked white
and ill. Mayne had told him plainly what forces were
opposed to him, and he had agreed to abandon the

SPECIAL CONSTABLE PREPARING FOR THE WORST.—DRYING HIS GUNPOWDER
IN THE FRYING-PAN.

procession, although the meeting itself was to be per-
mitted. Now he had to explain this to those to whom he
had promised that he would lead the procession in the
first rank, even if he were shot down. 'My children,'
he began, 'you were told industriously that I would not
be amongst you today; well, I am here!' He spent a
considerable time detailing his own sufferings for the
cause. His physician had forbidden him to appear. He
had spent six sleepless nights in their service, and his

breast was like a coal of fire. His father had been tried
five times for high treason, his uncle was in the fifteenth
year of his banishment and was about to be made
President of France. 'My brother is Prime Minister and
Commander-in-chief of a Republic in South America.'
His speeches were always rambling, but this one seemed
to go on indefinitely. At last the crowd began to realize
that he was advising them not to go in procession to
Westminster. There were blessings in store for them
from the Chartist Land Company he had founded, and
he could not spare one of his children from the feast.

The Executive would escort the Petition; they need
not come too. He would go down on his knees to
implore them not to do so. 'If you want to kill me, my
life is at your command; but to others I will not surrender
it. Then there is another thing I wish you to remember
– I don't think you could well spare me just now.
(*Cheers and laughter*.)' Five million, seven hundred
thousand had signed. Was not that enough? The
strange and inconsequent stream of words went on; the
audience was first depressed, then puzzled, and then
acquiescent. Ernest Jones followed with a speech to the
same effect; it was getting towards two o'clock and the
audience was tired; Reynolds and Harney, who spoke
next, were not well listened to. The Executive drove off
with the Petition in three cabs; O'Connor duly presented
it to the House.

The crowd at the Common had dispersed, mostly no
doubt merely disappointed and uncertain, but some of
the younger men had prepared for a fight and were in
an angry mood; they seem to have intended to make
some sort of an attempt at least.[94] Moreover, by now
even the plumper special constables were feeling valiant;

there were all the elements of a conflict, and it began. There was ugly scuffling on Blackfriars Bridge as some of the Chartists returned. On Bankside on the south side there began organized fighting between the police and 'roughs'; Millais was involved in it and his more prudent friend, Holman Hunt, pulled him away with some difficulty. The two artists went round by London Bridge, the Bank and Holborn, where they found 'agitators' were very active. But the incipient disorder was literally washed away; the clouds which had been lowering all day broke in steady, heavy London rain. Neither the exasperated revolutionaries nor the exultant specials wanted after a few minutes to charge up and down the streets breaking each other's heads. They wanted to shelter in porches and doorways, and ultimately, since the rainstorm would not stop, to go back to their homes or command-posts. There were many reasons why there could be no successful revolutionary coup in London on April 10th, 1848; which reasons were the more profound depends upon whether the systems of Engels, Spengler, Toynbee or Usher be taken as a guide. But there was only one reason why there was no attempt; it was rain.

The House of Commons had ordered the signatures to the Petition to be counted forthwith; thirteen law clerks had done so and the Committee reported that there were not 5,700,000 signatures. There were exactly 1,975,496. Moreover, many of these signatures were suspect, as, for example, the Duke of Wellington and Queen Victoria, Davy Jones and Mr. Punch, Flatnose and No Cheese, and obscene names with which (said the reporter) he would not offend the House or its dignity. O'Connor rose in a rage, and said the figures were false and no clerks could have counted two million signatures in the time. William Cripps, a member of the Committee, answered even more passionately; claiming that he did not wish 'to throw obloquy and ridicule' on O'Connor, he nevertheless went on to say that he 'ought to be deprived of every credence to which man was entitled. I will never believe him again.' The Petition was 'a ribald mass of obscenity and impiety'. Both men had lost their self-control; a duel was only prevented by the intervention of the Speaker and the temporary arrest of O'Connor.[95] The House was shaken and disquieted; it would have been more so, perhaps, had it known of another circumstance. Both men were going mad. Cripps died within a month of what was called 'a brain fever'. O'Connor's decay took longer, but before long he could be seen at dawn wandering around Covent Garden, a great, shambling figure with his arms hanging down like an ape's, his eyes glazed and his hair white, sometimes picking up a fruit or vegetable and smiling or laughing over it fatuously. This was the man who believed he was the descendant of the High Kings of Ireland, who had expected to become the first President of the British Republic – whom, indeed, more people had wished to put in that office than had voted for the House of Commons which defeated him.

That the other side had been frightened it now denied; but the Duke of Wellington recorded the facts with his usual unsentimental exactness in the House of Lords the day after April 10th. He used the words, 'the terror of this great meeting which had been called. It was to have consisted, it was said, of 200,000 people. God knows how many thousands did attend, but still the effect was to place all the inhabitants of the metropolis under alarm, paralysing all trade and business of every description and driving individuals to seek safety by arming themselves for the protection of their lives and those of their neighbours and the security of their property.'

Lord John Russell, the Premier, had been under so great a strain that the birth of his second son three days later seemed to combine with the passing of this threat to bring a fresh world to him. He celebrated this in a

Lord John Russell

poem bringing in the unfortunate pet name he had chosen for the little boy:

Wi' the violet and gowan he breathed his first breath,
They smile, and grim winter disarmèd we see;
To our country, still echoing danger and death
Like a cherub of peace came my bonny Wee-wee.[96]

Their denial, or rather their disbelief, that they had ever been seriously scared has helped to falsify the picture painted by later historians. This is to the effect

that the menace was serious, the victory tremendous
and final, and the Chartist failure total and ridiculous.
The Chartist movement was 'laughed off the stage'; it
disappeared promptly and for ever, and with it ended
the age of nonsense and began that of Victorian stability.
The two earliest, and still the best, histories of Chartism
actually end their story with this month of April. But
history is rarely as conveniently theatrical as that; when
later accounts are compared with the day-to-day record
in newspapers and diaries a more complex picture is
seen. There was no great victory on April 10th;
O'Connor's bargain with Mayne was a compromise
– he held the banned meeting at the price of foregoing
the procession. There was nothing unusually ridiculous
in the signatures to the Petition: all politicians knew that
petitions which lay open for signature for some time
always included a proportion of practical jokes beginning
with F or B.[97] It was only the boasting of O'Connor,
like the fear of his enemies, which was excessive to the
point of the ridiculous. Nor did the Chartist movement
disappear; it came back within the year in some quite
serious activities. Nor, finally, was this the end of
'nonsense'; some most engaging nonsense filled the
British scene for months to come.

As usual, it was women's activities which most amused
the Victorians. There were a few active feminine
revolutionaries among the Chartists, but the sex as a
whole was loyal. A number of them attended the
special constables as a kind of highly respectable
vivandières, in wide skirts which were short enough to
show little laced bootees beneath. Some wished to be
enrolled as constables themselves; they were easy meat
for the cartoonists, who drew them in top-hats and with

staves, fainting against each other when spoken to roughly. *Punch*,[98] parodied feminist claims by printing a 'Maid's Charter' ('That unlimited pocket money shall begin at 16. . . . That when the marriage is solemnized the DUKE OF WELLINGTON shall give away the bride') and a 'Wife's Charter' – 'That the honeymoon shall last six months. . . . That the husband invariably smoke in

ORIGIN OF THE FONETIC MYSTERY.

the garden (if no garden, no smoke). . . . That the DUKE OF WELLINGTON be godfather to the first child.'

A clear-headed and competent young business-man, who afterwards was Sir Isaac Pitman and the inventor of the most successful and profitable of shorthands, decided that the time was now ripe for the substitution of a rational phonetic alphabet for the current one. His *Fʊnetic Jurnal* was so successful that – signing ✠zac Pitman – he was able to call in BERMINAM the SICSɪ ANQAL FʊNETIC FESTIVAL as a result of which (he felt sure) there would be published next year a phonetic NQZPAPER which would drive out of existence *The Times* and other journals which adhered to an old irrational spelling. There were reports of sweeping enthusiasm from YⴀRC, from CEΓ in Bamf∫er and from the ⴕl ov Man, where a Mr. Σerifs had a f8nt ov fⴍnotips and printed in them sum ov δe Sqmz. (What Mr. Sheriffs of the Isle of Man had printed in his phonotypes was 'some of the Psalms'; the other places that so strongly supported Mr. Pitman and his two brothers Ben and 'Henri' were York, and Keith in Banffshire.)⁹⁹

J. Goodwin Barmby, a clergyman who afterwards became a Unitarian, had organized a Communist Church and ran a Communist paper which seems to have disappeared, though it had some considerable influence. The word 'communist' was used in the original sense of 'strict community of all goods'.¹⁰⁰ The Concordium, another society which sprung into eminence, was slightly less austere. Its members were allowed to retain a little individual property, but they had to submit themselves strictly to the rule of their 'Pater', William Oldham, who had occupied this post since 1842. He was leading them gently upon the road to a higher life. They first were deprived of alcohol, and then of meat. Having become strict vegetarians they had now been put on a diet of unfired foods and cold water only. Their doctrine was a mixture of Pantheism and Socialism, and they were instructed to abandon marriage in favour of a system of sexual intercourse based on arithmetical and rational regulations (which unfortunately are not more exactly described). Over the winter they had been deprived of underclothes, shoes and stockings, as a preparation, their Pater said, to a life of complete nudity. Both April and May were very cold this year, and in particular abominably rainy; the members reacted variously to the weather. Some ignobly left the Concordium and put on warm pants or stays; James Elmslie Duncan, their secretary, got himself locked in jail for holding up the traffic in Bishopsgate by reciting his own revolutionary poems; but the majority reconstituted themselves as 'The Tropical Emigration Society', and moved en masse to Venezuela, presumably as the warmest Republic which accepted emigrants of even the oddest views.[101]

Rather less dramatic, but much more important, were the activities of another religious group – Charles Kingsley the novelist, Ludlow, Maurice, Hughes, Neale and others who invented for themselves the name 'Christian Socialists'. They put up posters urging the Chartists who were discontented with the results of April 10th to substitute for such meetings their programme of the foundation of Co-operative productive societies on a Christian basis. They had, to all appearances, very little success; indeed, their propaganda seemed well calculated to perplex their audience. 'To call men to repentance first of all,' wrote Maurice, 'and then also, as it seems to me, to give them the opportunity of showing their repentance and bringing forth fruits of it – this is my idea of a Tailors' Association.' Yet they were less absurd and unimportant than they seemed. Bishop Phillpotts was a great man then and the Rev. Charles Kingsley a nobody; but 100 years later the strength of the two ideas they represented in their Church had been almost transposed. It is partly due to them, too, that neither in England nor anywhere else in the Commonwealth did there appear the Continental type of 'Christian Socialist party', a thing whose behaviour is

unchristian and whose programmes are unsocialist;
nor has there ever been a break between organized
labour and organized religion.[102]

The columns of newspapers seemed more frivolous and
less oppressed by politics. They had room to notice an
epitaph in a Winchester churchyard:

To the Memory of Thomas Fletcher

Here sleeps in peace a Hampshire Grenadier
Who caught his death by drinking cold small beer;
Soldiers, be wise from his untimely fall
And when ye're hot drink strong or none at all,

and to record that the officers of the regiment, observing
that the inscription was decaying, had had it recut and
added:

An honest soldier never is forgot
Whether he die by musket or by pot.

They were deliciously shocked, at the very end of the
month, by the commencement of a case which suggested
widespread licence in aristocratic houses. 'Romping
usual in noblemen's establishments' ran the headline.[103]
John Shores, the butler in a Marquis's house, 12 Carlton
Gardens, was sued for an affiliation order by Hannah
Knott, a 'well-looking young woman' with a baby in her
arms, who had been a housemaid under his control in
June, 1847. While the family was out of town, the
butler had come upon her when she was doing the
bedrooms. 'Let us see,' he had said, 'if the beds are
properly made,' and had then 'effected her ruin'. What,
in one of the family's bedrooms? No; not being wholly
lost to propriety, he had carried her to his own room.
The butler did not contest the story, but claimed the

child was not his; the girl was common to all on the staff. He had footmen ready to swear to this; his lawyer called the first footman, Thomas Nicholson, who at first alleged that he had enjoyed her often; but under examination he broke down, abandoned the pretence and was warned of the penalty for perjury. William Worsum, second footman, at this determined to tell only the truth and said that he had romped with her, in the manner that was 'usual in all noblemen's establishments', but it was harmless. The magistrate, Mr. Hardwick, was one of those who could not leave well alone. What was this romping? Chasing the maids in corridors and smaller rooms. 'To snatch a kiss?' (benignly). More usually, on the pretext of an offence to throw up their skirts and chastise their persons with the hand; to fondle them; to—— The footman went on to elaborate; the magistrate stopped him and granted the order.

V

May

*

MAY: in their relief from their anxieties the readers of the English papers could even think of art. Descriptions of painting, for the first few days, took almost as much space as news of foreign affairs or even of Parliament. Alexis Soyer opened at 209 Regent Street in London the exhibition of the works of his 'wife and departed angel', Emma. As he had expected, the influential and the rich made a point of going to it, paying £250 in entrance fees, which provided no less than 50,000 meals at the Spitalfields kitchen which he was running, and where as many as 350 destitute people were turning up daily. The Reform Club members and the others paid their entrance money cheerfully enough, but found it less easy to praise the paintings; at last one 'eminent critic' was able to tell the press that there was a portrait of a dog among them which would 'do no discredit to Mr. Landseer'.[104]

The praise may seem to us slight or even absurd; it was not. It was the highest approval that could be given. For the exhibition at the Royal Academy which opened in the first days of May showed Edwin Landseer, by a series of partly fortuitous circumstances, as the foremost artist in Great Britain – and therefore, as few doubted in those days before the supremacy of Paris, as the foremost in the world. All his possible rivals fell away from him, and he was seen in this show on a lonely and unattainable eminence. There was obviously one man who might have equalled and even outdone him. But J. M. W. Turner, as so often, was sulking. He had for years hidden his natural kindness and good sense (though not his genius) under a coating of moroseness, meanness and dirt; he lived in the suburbs under the name of Admiral Booth in a filthy house where a guest was likely to be offered sherry out of a cracked teacup if anything. When he spoke, he mumbled; when he was audible he was incomprehensible. He wore a wrapper over his head and another round his throat.

> His short figure had become corpulent, his face, perhaps from continual exposure to the air, was unusually red and a little inclined to blotches. His dark eye was bright and restless, his nose aquiline. He generally wore what is called a black dress coat which would have been the better for brushing – the sleeves were mostly too long, coming down over his fat and not overclean hands.[105]

There was even some relief at the news that he had, for no reason given, refused to exhibit anything at all at the Academy this year. The *Athenaeum*, the most acute critic of the day, missed 'his creative and soaring power', but added that he had 'taxed our credulity'. Others who might have challenged Landseer were also excluded by their own action. Two Irish painters, Maclise and Mulready, were thought to be almost as great – indeed, W. P. Frith who afterwards painted 'Derby Day', assures us that the former was regarded as 'out and away the greatest artist that ever lived'. But they presented this year nothing of importance; an attempt was made to claim that Mulready's 'The Butt' was 'the picture of the year', but it would not do. It represented a boy, escorted by two girls, dropping cherries into the mouth of a butcher's errand-boy; it seemed pointless. Etty was brilliant, and was the one painter for whom Victorian prudery was wholly suspended; 'he saw naked girls as sinuous animals with silken skins', writes R. H. Wilenski,[106] but, alas! this year he chose to exhibit a disappointingly clothed 'Group of Captives by the Waters of Babylon' which had 'charms of colour' but wholly lacked what was euphemistically called 'his niceties of form'. Younger men had not yet reached Landseer's level; Frith, who was to succeed to his reputation, was moderately praised for 'broad humour conveyed without vulgarity' and G. F. Watts's picture of M. Guizot was dismissed as 'not successful'.

The *Athenaeum*, from which these comments are mostly taken, made a slight effort to struggle against the victory of Landseer. 'If anything can reconcile us to seeing Art employed in epigrammatizing a high moral, it must be such a success as Mr. Landseer's', it wrote, and referred to the 'canine physiognomies, for which this artist is utterly unapproached'.[107] The grudging praise was elicited by the greatest picture in the exhibition, 'Alexander and Diogenes', which was, of course, bought by the National Gallery. It showed Alexander as a big white bulldog, visiting a miserable cur as Diogenes. Alexander was 'knitting his brows' and lifting an eyebrow in a rather uncanine way; almost every other known kind of dog stood around to represent the courtiers. But the second greatest picture was not limited to dogs; it represented a doe shot dead upon a snowy hillside, with a fawn nuzzling it to find the milk that would never flow again; and lest any critic should miss the moral the title A RANDOM SHOT was set out in large capitals below.[108] It was perverse, indeed, to refuse to admit Landseer's greatness; it had been sealed by more important judges than an anonymous journalist. In 1840 Queen Victoria and Prince Albert themselves had thought it worth while to etch 'certain designs' of his, and had entertained themselves the same way in 1841, in 1842, in 1843 and in 1844. The Government had asked him to paint three hunting scenes for the Peers' Refreshment Room in the new Houses of Parliament, which he had agreed to do for £500 each.[109] He knew his own importance; his manner was already superb, though not as arrogant as it was to become. When he was 'visitor' for the Life School of the Academy, he would keep the students locked out for half an hour or three-quarters while he 'placed' the model; yet, when they entered, he would turn his back on them and read a newspaper, neither speaking to them nor looking at their work until he ended the class by walking out. They contrasted his behaviour angrily with that of Turner, smelling, shuffling, rubbing their efforts with a grubby thumb, muttering obscurely, but intending to be helpful and, on the rare occasions when he was comprehensible, as illuminating as lightning.[110]

The apotheosis of mediocrity, the enthronement of a Landseer flanked by Maclise and Mulready, the tone and quality of almost every picture hung on the walls this year provoked a revolt which in time was to destroy everything which it attacked – and in its turn to be attacked and destroyed for almost the same faults which it found in the Academy. The instrument of this revolt was the Pre-Raphaelite Brotherhood, founded this year, with some friends, by the two young men who had got themselves entangled in the Chartist demonstration. It was aided by the encouragement and financial help of a man who was made an A.R.A. – Associate of the Royal Academy – this year, but whose name almost forbids the thought that he could be artistically or historically of importance. He was called Augustus Egg.

Egg lived in Ivy Cottage, a comfortable house behind a public house named the Black Lion in what is now the Queen's Road, Bayswater. His accent was undignified – he visited Belgium 'viar-Ostend' and he dropped his initial 'Ys'; but his house was a regular meeting place for discussions on art, and for useful dinners with likely patrons.[111] He was moderately well off, and would purchase his young friends' works for £25 or £50, but, more importantly, forced his wealthier acquaintances to buy them at higher prices. Holman Hunt had painted a 'Rienzi' which incarnated all the principles of the new school and which the most competent critic he knew had told him would be better balanced if hung upside down. Egg, at the height of Hunt's natural depression, sold it by mere pertinacity for a full £100 to a collector who detested it so much that he shut it in a cupboard where it could not be seen.[112] He even prevented Frith losing his money at thimble-rig at the Derby, by calling in the police. He himself exhibited pictures well above average merit; this year his 'Queen Elizabeth discovers she is no longer young', showed 'more than his accustomed strength';[113] following on page 144 are reproductions of three of his best paintings.

The founders of the Pre-Raphaelite Brotherhood whom he helped were few and young. Holman Hunt was just twenty-one. John Millais was two years younger. His contemporaries sourly called him the Infant Prodigy;

he was dazzlingly handsome with bright curly hair, schoolboyish in manners, spoiled by his parents, alternating between charm and petulance, and already inordinately skilled in painting technique. The idea of the Brotherhood, it seems, started with these two alone; Hunt records long, stilted speeches which he says they made to each other advocating 'irreverent, heretical and revolutionary views'.[114] Within a month or two a convert of more powerful personality moved in on them – literally so, for Dante Gabriel Rossetti came into Hunt's studio, taking a bedroom in the same house. It was his demoniac energy (alternating with total idleness) that ran them into making an organized society, deciding formally on its principles, keeping it secret and using the signature P.R.B. as a private sign, and holding monthly meetings at which the young artists discussed and praised each other's works and projects. Among them was Woolner, a promising young sculptor, Collinson, a 'painstaking young draughtsman' who fell asleep longer and more often than Pickwick's Fat Boy, William Rossetti, who could not be refused because he was Gabriel's brother, although he already seemed 'a bloody fool' (the phrase of William Morris, a later arrival), F. G. Stephens who had as yet done nothing, but was pulled in by Hunt mostly because, if Rossetti had a dumb dependant, he would like to have one too, and some others now forgotten. Part of their revolt was youthful exuberance, expressed in all-night walks over Hampstead Heath shouting and singing, in re-christening Sir Joshua Reynolds 'Sir Sloshua', in drawing up a list of Immortals 'which constitutes the whole of our Creed, and there exists no other Immortality than what is centred in their names and in the names of their contemporaries'.

The names were marked with stars, as if they had been hotels in *Baedeker*; Jesus Christ had four stars and Shakespeare three; no one else had more than two.[115]

Jesus Christ****
The Author of Job**
Isaiah
Homer**
Pheidias
Early Gothic Architects
Cavaliere Pugliesi
Dante**
Boccaccio*
Rienzi
Ghiberti
Chaucer**
Fra Angelico*
Leonardo da Vinci**
Spenser
Hogarth
Flaxman
Milton
Goethe**
Kosciusko
Byron
Wordsworth
Keats**
Shelley**
Haydon
Cervantes
Joan of Arc
Mrs. Browning*
Patmore*

Raphael*
Michael Angelo
Early English Balladists
Giovanni Bellini
Georgione
Titian
Tintoretto
Poussin
Alfred**
Shakespeare***
Milton
Cromwell
Hampden
Bacon
Newton
Landor**
Thackeray**
Poe
Hood
Longfellow*
Emerson
Washington**
Leigh Hunt
Author of *Stories after Nature**
Wilkie
Columbus
Browning**
Tennyson*

Why was Dickens excluded and Thackeray kept in? Who was the author of *Stories After Nature*? There is no answer to these questions, for the members were in later life a little ashamed of the list, more for its 'atheistical' preface than its oddity.

But the Brotherhood was by no means all youthful nonsense, or it would not have ended by knocking the Landseer-Mulready school out of power and almost out of existence. They had realized what far more acute critics had missed – that in 1848 English art was in fact dead, that, apart from Turner (who was to die in two years' time), there was hardly a painter whose work was not derivative and dishonest. Hunt, the most articulate of them, had already explained this to Rossetti:

> I showed him my new picture of 'Rienzi' in the painting of which at the outset I was putting in practice the principle of rejection of conventional dogma and pursuing that of direct application to Nature for each feature, however humble a part of foreground or background this might be. I justified the doing of this thoroughly as the only sure means of eradicating the stereotyped tricks of decadent schools.[116]

The Pre-Raphaelites were 'art naturalists'; that is, they were returning to the honest tradition of clear observation of nature. After examining some engravings of the frescoes of Benozzo Gozzoli in the Campo Santo at Pisa, the date when this tradition was broken became clear to them; it was the date of the death of Raphael.[117] Raphael himself was a genius, but his followers, the Raphaelites, 'accentuated his poses into postures, caricatured the turns of his heads and lines of his limbs so that figures were drawn in patterns',[118] and thus had imposed conventions still obeyed – such as that that all figures in a picture must have their places on a line shaped like the letter S, that the parts of a composition should be apexed in pyramids, that one corner must always be in shade, and so forth. The effect of all this upon contemporary art was fairly accurately shown in Hunt's description of the pictures chosen by the Royal Academy:

> Every scene was planned as for the stage, with second rate actors to play the parts, striving to look less like sober live men than pageant statues of waxwork. Knights were frowning and staring as none but hired supernumeraries could stare; the pious had vitreous tears on their reverential cheeks; innkeepers were ever round and redfaced; peasants had complexions of dainty pink; homely couples were ever reading a Family Bible in a circle of most exemplary children.[119]

There is but one hesitation to be felt over this admirable denunciation; it reads strangely like a venomous description of some of the later works of the Pre-Raphaelites themselves. Nothing could be much more artificial than the unending series of costume pieces by Rossetti, Millais and Hunt, entitled 'Arthur's Tomb', 'Banquet Scene from Keats' *Isabella*', 'Christians escaping from Druid Persecution', 'Sir Isumbras at the Ford' and so forth. Nor could there be a flatter example of 'epigrammatizing a high moral' than the picture which Hunt himself felt to be the *chef-d'œuvre* of the movement. It is called 'The Light of the World' and shows a middle-aged man in a nightgown with the sort of expression that a modern schoolgirl calls 'soppy', holding a kind of

Chinese lantern; it hangs in Keble College, Oxford, and visitors paid and perhaps still do pay a small sum for the privilege of seeing it.

But these were in the future: for the moment pictures signed P.R.B. were in colours denounced as garish, contained figures standing about anyhow instead of in capital S's, were brilliantly accurate in detail, and if they had for our taste too many moralizing or pseudo-historical subjects were much less so afflicted than their rivals'. They were a harmonious part, that is, of a year which was still a year of revolution. For the failure of the Chartists the month before did not mean the defeat of the revolutionary spirit. It meant only that it had been circumscribed; April 10th had said 'No farther' to the revolution politically, but that was all. There was not going to be a World Federation of Free Republics. Revolutionary expansion had been stopped at Kennington Common in London and there was no other country to which the revolutionaries could turn. The United States was, by definition, perfect already (except for the slave states). Russia, Turkey and China were dead and barbarous empires. What happened in Latin America even earnest revolutionaries agreed was of no importance. Once the specials and the Duke had stopped the British revolution there were no fresh political successes to be expected. That did not, however, mean that the gains made would be lost. The coming months might well be months of consolidation. The French, the Prussians, the Bavarians, the Austrians, the Hungarians, the Danes and the Italians could establish and enjoy the freedom that they had achieved.

But to establish freedom is neither so easy nor (in some ways) so entertaining as to achieve it; in particular, the interest and enthusiasm of the Italians, a drama-loving people, was waning throughout May. Charles Albert, the King of Piedmont, had insisted upon his plebiscite in Lombardy; it was held on May 15th and on May 28th resulted, of necessity, in an application ('granted as soon as asked') to be annexed to Piedmont. Mazzini and his fellow Republicans denounced the trick angrily; it took some of the heart out of the Italian war on Austria. For it was war; the Austrian Marshal Radetzky had recovered from the shock and was fighting back, though at present with little success. Charles Albert gave curiously little assistance to the Venetians, who had not yet asked to be annexed; he spent his time besieging the big Austrian fort of Peschiera; but in the end he took it. The Pope in effect had withdrawn his troops, such as they were, from the conflict; his pronouncements seemed to contradict those of his ministers, but both were vague. Worse happened in Naples further south; King Ferdinand called his armies home from the Austrian war, cancelled his constitution and on May 15th drove out the Parliament. Treachery was to be expected of him; what was more sinister was that he had the support of 'the people' in his action. The proletariat of Naples, called the *lazzaroni*, was as cruel and greedy as an Arab mob, and even more superstitious; but it had been believed that anywhere the call of liberty and equality would be answered by something honest and healthy in the deep heart of any people. For the first time civilized men, of middle or working class alike, found that this was not so. The King turned the *lazzaroni* on them; 'Naples is yours' he is reported to have said.[120] There were some hours of robbery, outrage, and murder; then there was nothing left of the

Neapolitan revolution. The King now had leisure to
plan the reconquest of Sicily, also nominally part of his
dominions; the Sicilians felt it wise to ask Charles
Albert's son, the Duke of Genoa, to become their King.

The news from Germany was equally uninspiring; it
was neither on the whole good nor bad; it was con-
fusing there too. There was something missing; something had gone from the atmosphere. The Germans,
with their romantic mysticism, sensed this more even
than the Italians. It appears that there is a feeling of
revolution; there is a sensation which is almost a
physical one of being part of a sudden and profound
change. It was one that was felt fairly frequently in
Europe from 1789 onwards; it happens that a man of
genius, a German, recorded it. Richard Wagner was in
Dresden when he heard the tocsin suddenly ring out
from the Church of St. Ann in the Postplatz, and knew
what it meant.

> It was a very sunny afternoon [he wrote] and I at
> once noticed the same phenomenon as Goethe
> describes in his attempt to depict his own sensations
> during the bombardment of Valmy. The whole
> square looked as though it was illuminated by a
> dark yellow, almost brown light, such as I had once
> before seen in Magdeburg during an eclipse of the
> sun. My most pronounced sensation beyond this
> was one of great, almost extravagant satisfaction.
> I felt a sudden strange longing to play with some-
> thing hitherto regarded as dangerous and im-
> portant.[121]

There were few such moments in Germany now. The
new Parliament was sitting in Frankfurt and it was

debating the means of setting up a new German State and the character of that State. It would have to include a large number of now independent powers. There were two of them, Austria and Prussia, of equal importance. Would one submit to the other? What would be the position of the possessions that they both had which were traditionally outside Germany? The problem was one of great complexity, and debates were bound to be prolonged and tiring. Moreover, the Parliament House, St. Paul's Church, was very inconvenient although much money had been spent on preparing it. The members sat tightly packed in seats to which there were few and narrow gangways, as if it had been a theatre, and looked towards a sort of stage, on which was the President's chair and a pulpit for the speaker; above these two was a large symbolic picture of 'Germania', a blonde lady whose expression is described as innocent but weak-willed. The gangways were not nearly broad enough for members to stop and talk, especially when their numbers rose from 320 to 586. There were no refreshment rooms or committee rooms at all. The galleries were occupied by spectators, who remembered that the success of the French Convention (as they had read) had been largely due to the intervention of the audience, shouting down or menacing with death any speaker whose views they disliked. Everything, that is, was arranged to encourage long, flowery and enthusiastic speeches on first principles, and to discourage practical discussions in committees or in private. For these the members, ministers and President included, had to travel 'some considerable distance' into the centre of the town, or stand in the open in the Church Square. Opinion was gravely offended by the practical alternative adopted by some members, of diving into one or other of the cheap public-houses nearby; the first German democratic Parliamentarians in the world ought not to have been seen so often hurrying out of low bars into the House, and then back again.[122]

The proceedings of the Parliament, in face of these difficulties, were far more sensible, dignified and encouraging than could have been expected. Ingenious writers, both from the Left and the Right, have since for their own separate reasons run this Parliament down and jeered at its members – mostly for the rather Germanic reason that eventually it was not stronger than its enemies. But as it is watched more closely, in its day to day performance, its credit rises steadily in the eye of the beholder. It had an admirable President in Heinrich von Gagern, dignified, impeccably honest, fair, and courteous except when a justified anger would frighten into silence a member who used his position to vent malice or rouse disorder. He had to deal with many unreasonable and far from House-trained speakers, from windbags on the Left to Prussian officers on the Right – such as the elegant Prince Lichnowsky, who specialized in provoking his opponents by interruptions which were as witty as they were insolent. If it was too inclined to interrupt its proceedings to pay homage to an elderly patriotic poet such as Arndt and to ask him to write from his 'good old German conscience' extra verses to his *What is the German's Fatherland?*, well, it would not have represented Germany nor retained German confidence if it had not occasionally indulged in an orgy of romantic sentiment. Even its cow-like ruminance of democratic philosophy was probably useful in a country which, unlike France, England or America, was politically totally uneducated. It had to decide whether the new Germany should be republican or monarchist; the majority decided for monarchy – probably rightly so, in view of the possibilities of the moment and the fact that every individual German state was still a monarchy. It was less easy to decide who the monarch should be; it was probably sensible for the moment to concentrate upon the writing of a constitution and in particular upon the defining of the rights of every German. That, after all, was what was most urgent; it was the personal tyrannies and humiliations which any officer or bureaucrat could inflict and had inflicted on the ordinary German which must be stopped. For this, the fundamental rights, the *Grundrechte*, must be defined, and a start was made on this.

The assembly was only inveigled into one intervention into current politics, and thereby tangled itself instantly in the complexities of German geography. The new, so-democratic King Frederick of Denmark was amusing his people with a patriotic adventure. He had decided to incorporate into Denmark the two duchies of Schleswig and Holstein, which he ruled as Duke; the second and southernmost was technically part of the German confederation and was also full of Germans. These Germans revolted and were put down by the Danes; they appealed to the King of Prussia, who with the assent of the Frankfurt assembly marched in some Prussian troops under a general named von Wrangel. Was it perhaps quite wise to send the Prussian army out on such an exercise? The members did not ask themselves this question; they roared out *What is the German's Fatherland?* over again, without its new verse, in voices shaken by tears of pride. It would have been unreasonable to expect them to do anything else. Could the first German congressmen watch silently while Germans were oppressed by Danes? Was the calling of the first German Parliament to be the signal for second-rate powers pinching pieces of the Fatherland? Had not King Frederick William promised loyalty to liberty and Germany, and indeed shown it by his prompt invasion of Holstein? Finally, had not recent events shown that it would be as well to restore some power and prestige to police forces and armies? The rapidly retreating rumps of Frau Herwegh and Dr. Hecker were in more senses than one a sight not easily forgotten.

The most significant of all the events of this May occurred, as usual, in Paris; but its significance was not in the least plain at the time. It seemed not much more than a noisy and stupid scuffle – so stupid, indeed, that there are those who still believe it was a trap into which the revolutionaries walked.

The elections to the Assembly had been held, and had resulted in a heavy defeat for what was now coming to be called the Socialist group. 'Communist' was a word used for advocates of 'communities' like the English Concordium; the word 'socialist' also was used in a sense different from today's and meant no more than someone who whatever his programme was on the side of those who wore the 'blouse' (working clothes, used as jeans or boiler-suits are today) against those who wore the 'habit' or town suit. The large majority of the Assembly was indeed Republican (the monarchists being hopelessly divided between Legitimists and Orleanists), but these Republicans considered that the Revolution had gone quite far enough, that property and order must now be secured, and that plans like Louis Blane's for the 'organization of labour' and attempts by the Paris proletariat to overawe the Government must now both vanish into the realm of the un-unthinkable. They marked their opinion by re-electing the Government much as it was, but striking off Louis Blanc and the gas-worker Albert. Blanc, searching like Ledru Rollin and Lamartine for a revolutionary proto-type, had by now cast himself for the role of Robespierre which was as suitable as if the late Sidney Webb had tried to model himself on Cromwell. He addressed the Assembly sternly and demanded that his programme should be adopted and he should be appointed a Minister of Labour – an unheard-of office. The motion was rejected with rude comments and a large majority; the rejection was not merely a snub to an ambitious journalist but, because of the Workers' Commission at the Luxembourg which had backed him, an insult to a large section of the Paris working class. It was so intended. Nor were Blanc's supporters the only section with a grievance against the Assembly. Ledru-Rollin was still a member of the Government but his supporters, including Mme. Aurore in her paper, were threatening again to dissolve 'the false national representation' if it did not 'obey the people's will'. The leaders of a dozen or so of the political clubs were earnestly discussing similar propositions almost daily; they were also jockey-ing for position among each other. If there was a chance of a new Provisional Government coming to power as one had done in February, they did not intend to be left out this time. The prefect of police, Marc Caussidière, was on affectionate terms with nearly all of them. The ablest of them all, the fanatic who looked_like a corpse,

Auguste Blanqui, was on good terms with none. His reputation had just been tarnished by a charge of having once been an informer, but a very large number of Paris workers valued him above anyone else, for his relentless devotion, his cynical humour, and his detestation of the gush and floridity of almost every other politician.[123]

The explosion came on May 15th. The Club leaders had decided on a demonstration that day in favour of Poland. Paris was full of Polish refugees, including a number who had gone to Posen after King Frederick William had invited them back to freedom, had found themselves engaged in the old struggle between Germans and Poles, and had seen the Poles defeated; the Parisian workers were very sympathetic with them. The Club leaders assured the Mayor of Paris that the demonstration would be unarmed; nevertheless, the amateur general de Courtais who was in charge was instructed to make sure that the Assembly was properly protected. He made careful plans to that end, but did not see that they were carried out. The prefect of police, Caussidière, was suffering from a bad knee all day on May 15th and took no action of any kind; his affliction disappeared suddenly the next morning. Therefore, when the demonstration reached the bridge leading to the Chamber, there were practically no forces to hold it back. It was much larger than was expected, and de Courtais lost his head. He first rode up and down in front of it, waving a Polish flag and shouting, '*Vive la Pologne!*' 'We respect your white hairs,' said one of the demonstrators, 'but we are going to enter the Chamber.' De Courtais, for reasons which are still uncertain, then ranged the troops that he had on the pavement, leaving the centre of the bridge unoccupied. Blanqui, who had

joined the demonstration rather sceptically, now decided
that it was serious and the people of Paris were really on
the move. He called out 'Forward!' in his hard, clear
voice, and, headed by his Club members, the crowd swept
on to the Chamber.[124]

Here there was a fantastic muddle whose details are
still uncertain. The deputies held their seats, but the hall,
the gallery, any vacant seats and the tribune were packed
with demonstrators, shouting slogans about Poland,
and starting and abandoning speeches. The Speaker
kept putting his hat on and off, to indicate that the
House was adjourned or not adjourned. He was able to
send out a note secretly to a less witless general than de
Courtais instructing him to beat the *rappel* – that is, the
Fall In – for the National Guard to come and rescue
Parliament. The demonstrators' speeches got more and
more furious, demanding an immediate declaration of
war on Russia and Prussia unless they freed Poland.
Blanqui tried to bring some reality into the shouting;
he added to this a demand for work for the unemployed,
and began to talk about 'the social causes of poverty'.
'Never mind about that!' shouted Sobrier, a club leader
who had a little police force of his own. 'Poland!
Poland! Talk about Poland.' Blanqui's intervention
had roused a more vehement rage in another leader,
Barbès, 'a Gascon and a Creole', the most emotional and
romantic speaker of them all, who detested him as a
personal rival. He rushed to the tribune, demanded that
the Assembly should immediately send an army to
Poland and put a tax of 1,000 million francs on the rich.
At that moment he heard a drum beat. 'Who has
sounded the Fall In?' he shouted. 'We are betrayed!
Hors la loi les traitres!' The Speaker was knocked over;

the House became a milling mass; in a few minutes a man called Hubert who had once been connected with the police called out, 'The Assembly is dissolved!' The deputies ran away.

It was now four o'clock, and Barbès marched off to the Hotel de Ville – that is, the Town Hall and the traditional place for the proclaiming of revolutionary governments. Most of the demonstrators left with him, and when the National Guard arrived half an hour later the Chamber was practically empty. But they did not continue with him – Blanqui called his followers off, thinking this was dangerous nonsense, Sobrier went off with a group to seize the Ministry of the Interior, the workers from the National Workshops went back to the bureau to draw their wages. 'Where is the people?' said Barbès, a little uncomfortably looking behind him; nevertheless, accompanied by the gas-worker Albert and a few hundred demonstrators, he pushed on. The guard on the Hotel de Ville let them in, because it remembered what had happened to those who had been unseasonably loyal in February. (The reason it offered at the enquiry later, however, was that the insurrection-aries showed official passes at the doors.) Barbès and Albert announced the members of the new Government (themselves, Sobrier, Caussidière, and a few others, but not Blanqui), declared war on Russia, and were preparing some other decrees when a violent uproar arose outside. After a short struggle, an officer of the National Guard broke into Barbès's room saying, 'Who are you?'

'A member of the Provisional Government.'

'Yesterday's or today's Government?'

'Today's.'

'Then I arrest you.'

Albert ran after them: 'If he is guilty, arrest me too!' The officer and his patrol did so. Most of the revolutionary forces had disappeared. It was five o'clock. Throughout the affair the Mayor, a man called Marrast, had been working on his papers undisturbed in a room down the corridor.[125]

During the night most of the club leaders were arrested. Caussidière was ordered out of the Prefecture of police, but he held to it like a leech, and it took a fortnight to get rid of him. Trials would follow in some months' time; but, meanwhile, surely everything could be considered as over. The Government, with clumsy good intentions, announced a Feast of Concord; it was from the beginning a failure. The detailed plans were absurd. Even the Archbishop of Paris refused to have anything to do with it, when he found the clergy were expected to parade behind a waggon drawn by cart-horses and labelled PROGRESS OF AGRICULTURE; the Parisian workers were very sarcastic at the expense of the statue of the Republic with four lions at its feet and the procession of 500 virtuous young women crowned with oak-leaves. The idea was no less absurd; there was no concord to celebrate. The National Assembly was as angry with the Government as the workers were angry with it. The assemblymen, indeed, had decided that if the Government was replaced by someone more vigorous it was certain that the threat from the Paris workers could be put an end to, finally and suddenly. The workers had no particular plan.

It was as yet unknown to either side, but in fact the escapade of May 15th had ended one era of revolutionary tactics, and opened another. Until that day, the classic formula of insurrection had been unchanged. All the revolutions of February and March had followed it; so had the various stages of the great French revolution; so, to some extent, had the more ancient examples of 1775 in America and 1649 in England. By this formula, revolution was a slow-maturing but spontaneous conflict between the people and the government. It was provoked by a series of oppressions which were resented by the people as a whole. There was no extensive organization of revolt; men united to explain to the people, by pamphlet and word of mouth, the outrageousness of the crimes practised; but that was all. They sacrificed themselves individually, and the words they spoke in court or on the scaffold rang through the nation. At the most, a single act might be concerted in the hope that it would spur the great mass to move. Tea might be thrown in a harbour, or troops defied so that they would shoot down the innocent. But these were sparks; all depended upon the natural explosion of the people, controlled, if at all, by the passionate speeches of its deputies. Once the people moved, the oppressors would be engulfed: the people was the immense majority and anyhow soldiers would not shoot their brothers. May 15th had shown that popular spontaneity was no longer enough; no Camille Desmoulins would ever again speak from a chair in the Palais Royal gardens and lead the people forthwith to storm a Bastille. A highly disciplined organization of revolutionary fighters must be formed, who would strengthen the loose popular masses as bones support a body. Occasions must be chosen which would suit the popular temper and would echo their real, not their temporary angers. Nothing must be done without careful preparation by calculating specialists. This was

the new formula, which was to be tried by Connolly in
Dublin in 1916 and Lenin in Petrograd in 1917. But in
Paris there was only one man as yet who appreciated it,
Blanqui, and now he was in prison.[126]

There seem to have been, however, men who had
realized this in London. The governing class there was
now at its ease, and it is doubtful if it suspected that an
essay in, or at least a rehearsal of the new tactic was
planned for May 29th.[127] The decaying influence, and
the decaying mind, of O'Connor had left the Chartist
leadership vacant; it was being taken over by more
determined men. Their names are uncertain. Cuffay
the mulatto was one, another was a doctor named
McDouall, another was a man called Fussell who had
killed a policeman off Gray's Inn Road some years
before; another wrote his memoirs thirty years later as
'Thomas Frost', but that was not his name. Historians
have been deceived by the small membership of the
National Charter Association, and have not realized
what large numbers those few men could direct. 'In
1848,' wrote 'Frost' of his own borough, 'there were in
Croydon about a dozen enrolled Chartists, and in the
village of Carshalton none; yet the Petition . . . was
signed in the former place by 2,000 men and in the latter
by 200 and I am able to testify to the genuineness of
every signature.' The enrolled men were by now
organized in 'wards' of ten by McDouall and Fussell,
and on the chosen date, which was a Monday, a large
proportion of them met in Clerkenwell Green in London,
where they were joined by Irishmen enraged by the
conviction of Mitchel, the ablest 'Young Ireland' speaker.
The words 'Fall In' and 'March' were given, and the
apparently disorganized mob formed columns of four

abreast and marched to Finsbury Square; here they met
more recruits, were re-formed in columns of twelve, and
marched westward. A hostile account gives their
numbers now as between 7,000 and 10,000.[128] They
continued westward, 'passwords being given at different
points', passing via Smithfield and Long Acre to
Leicester Square, where they halted. Afterwards, they
proceeded 'with a prodigious crowd' to Trafalgar
Square; they left soon afterwards without a conflict with
the police, being unarmed. 'Thomas Frost' gives their
numbers as 80,000 at the maximum; halve or quarter
the figure, it is still enormous for London in 1848, and
more than had been enough to overturn half a dozen
governments abroad. The whole day's proceedings were
extremely odd, and oddest of all was the indifference
with which the authorities apparently regarded them.

It may be that the indifference was more apparent
than real – later events suggest this – but certainly the
thoughts of the most powerful man in the Government
were far away from Chartism. Lord Palmerston's
policy was leading him into difficulties abroad; he
probably was never in his life embarrassed, but any other
man would have been, and his biographers have been
embarrassed for him. Yet there was nothing illogical in
his behaviour nor – if the fundamental reservations of
British policy are accepted – anything dishonourable
either. But he was accused of both faults, and even now
'feeble' is commonly the kindest word applied to British
policy in this year. This policy is most easily understood
if it is compared with the policy pursued by the American
Department of State in the thirties of this century, and
even to some extent in the forties. The Channel, in
Palmerston's day, was almost as much or as little a

barrier as the Atlantic is now; he also was in charge of the Foreign Office of one of the greatest powers in the world, which was partly isolated and would have preferred to be rather more so, but which also was emotionally involved in the fate of liberty abroad. He could not refrain, nor could his countrymen, from preaching to the governors and peoples of foreign countries and pointing out where they failed in courage, in love of liberty, in skill, or in common sense. He expressed warm and warmly felt interest in the fate of peoples who were struggling towards freedom; but those to whom he and other less careful Englishmen spoke did not understand the unspoken limitation to his encouragements. It was this: That the life of not a single British sailor or soldier would be risked in any circumstances. In this determination he was backed (as was later Mr. Hull) by the practically unanimous opinion of his countrymen. Throughout this year and the next, foreign Liberals and democrats, faced with the return of tyranny and barbarity, continually looked for a Palmerstonian stroke; it never came and never could have come. They reacted with bitter accusations of treachery, Pharisaism and cowardice; the English, who never understood why, found themselves with an international reputation for hypocrisy, selfishness and unreliability. They feted guiltily and lavishly the republican leaders who fled defeated to their shores; they could never understand the cold reserve with which their gifts and passionate speeches were received. There was nothing, they seemed to feel, that money and kind words could not set right.

Up to a certain point, Palmerston's sermons had their uses. Until it was realized that its words were only words, the remarks of the greatest naval power in the world were likely to be received with attention. Since last winter an itinerant missionary had been wandering round Germany and Italy advocating constitutionalism; his name was Lord Minto, he had the sinecure office of Lord Privy Seal, and was father-in-law to the Premier, Lord John Russell. He seemed to have had considerable success; he had even interviewed the Pope, but if that pontiff had really been influenced by him he was repenting rapidly.[129] Parliament was worried and rather displeased by the stories of this irregular diplomacy; this month it was more than displeased by the first of some lamentable affronts that Palmerston's strength in words and weakness in deeds were to bring. He had written on March 16th to the British Ambassador in Madrid a letter beginning in the following truly remarkable way:

> SIR, – I have to recommend you to advise the Spanish Government to adopt a legal and con-stitutional system. The recent downfall of the King of the French ought to indicate to the Spanish Court and Government the danger to which they expose themselves. . . .

The Ambassador, not a very bright one, transcribed this letter word for word and handed it to the Spanish Foreign Minister, the Duke de Sotomayor. The Duke was as professionally umbrageous as only a latter-day Spanish grandee can be; he had just disposed of the *liberales* and did not know or did not care that the *carlistas* would revolt in another part of the country in a week or two's time. He saw the opportunity for a long and, it could not be denied, effective answer, asking the Am-bassador how he would feel if the Spanish Cabinet

instructed Lord Palmerston's Government to behave
better towards the Irish and a number of other questions
which seemed pertinent as well as impertinent. He then
refused to receive the British note – which in those days
was an almost unprecedented piece of rudeness – and on
May 19th, realizing that the giant would not move,

A PROSPECT·OF·Yᵉ·VISCOVNTE
PALMERSTONE·PVTTVNGE HYS
FVTE·IN·IT.

ordered the Ambassador to leave Madrid. There was
nothing that the unhappy man could do but go.

Lord Palmerston's sympathy with the democrats in
Europe was limited, in a similar way as Mr. Hull's was a
century later with those who resisted Fascism and
Nazism. He saw with displeasure among them groups of
what were already called 'Reds', of whose programmes
he approved as little as did any Conservative. Their

importance was underlined and even exaggerated to him by an authority which was as difficult to define, constitutionally, as a Congressional Committee and certainly was more powerful. The Queen required more than access to files; she considered that she should approve any major despatch that Lord Palmerston sent out. Her chief adviser was her husband, Prince Albert, who might originally have sympathized a little with the proceedings of the Frankfurt Assembly, but who by now considered that the humiliation of German princes had gone too far, and in any case disliked Lord Palmerston and thought he should be taught to obey his Queen. She was affected, too, by Louis Philippe, the Prince of Prussia, Monsieur Guizot and the Prince von Metternich, people almost literally on her doorstep and almost literally bedraggled, whose sorrows were relayed to her by the sympathetic Princess Lieven. They might have had their faults, but it was clear to her now that her Foreign Secretary should have been using his influence merely to restore them to the positions which they had been so brutally deprived of. She was meditating, and shortly she sent, a letter in which she told him in typical phrases what she thought. She was '*ashamed*' of his policies, she told him. Particularly in Italy where instead of supporting the restoration of the Austrian Empire he was encouraging the setting up of a North Italian Kingdom under Charles Albert for the mean reason of 'gaining *influence* in Italy', a policy that had 'never done the *least good* in Spain, Portugal and Greece'. As for his idea of 'the establishment of an entente cordiale *with the French Republic*, for the purpose of driving the Austrians out of *their dominions* in Italy', why, that would be 'a *disgrace to this country*'.

But it would be a false picture of public opinion or even Her Majesty's opinion which showed it as mainly concerned with such problems. It was more interested in the christening this month of her fourth daughter, Louisa Caroline Alberta, at which a Chorale whose words and music were composed by Prince Albert was sung. This began:

> In life's gay morn, ere sprightly youth
> By vice and folly is enslaved,
> Oh, may thy Maker's glorious name,
> Be on thy infant mind engraved!

It was as interested by the appearance of Mr. Charles Dickens on the stage as Justice Shallow in *The Merry Wives of Windsor*, in which he excelled in 'the vacant stare, the complacent chuckle, and the wandering wonder of the eyes'. It was disagreeably shocked by the 'most determined suicide' of an M.P. named Redhead Yorke; the unhappy man had drunk cyanide, and a fellow M.P., Dr. Wakley, who acted as Coroner, said that he had had twelve drachms of water in his brain and for seven years, since he first arrived in the House of Commons, had not been 'altogether right in the head', although, of course, he was son-in-law of Lord Brandon.[130] Even for minds less given to sensationalism there were subjects more interesting than foreign imbroglios. Railroads were still strange things. Mr. G. M. Young has pointed out that 'there is no scene in a third-class railway carriage in Dickens';[131] but they were spreading rapidly in Britain and the United States, even if they had been halted elsewhere by political disorders. In the former country there was an army of 175,000 'navvies' and followers, going about the country

building them; 5,000 miles of them were finished and
2,000 miles in construction; the island, indeed, was now
joined up by a sort of gigantic iron cross centring on
Birmingham, so that a man could go from Bristol or
Dover to Lancaster or Newcastle without using a
horse.[132] There was, however, at the end of this month
an unexpected threat to them. That they were dangerous everyone knew; only a few weeks ago Markland, the
driver of an engine on the London and South Western

THE (PRESENT) WATERLOO STATION, YORK-ROAD.

Railway, had been killed while lying underneath his
engine and screwing on some parts which had fallen off,
and there were collisions almost every other month. But
it now appeared that there was a possibility that railways
might be checked, if not stopped, wherever there was a
river. The bridge over the Tyne belonging to the
Newcastle and Carlisle Railway was burnt to ashes,
having been ignited by sparks from the engine. The
suspension bridge over the Forth, at Meiklewood, fell
into the river owing to rot attacking the timbers. The

immense and beautiful railway bridge across the Usk in South Wales, which had been 'kyanized' to prevent rot, burst into flames, the kyanotic composition aiding the fire so that it soared like a great leaf into the air and destroyed £20,000 worth of construction in two hours. The river was black with burnt wood for miles. Unless, therefore, railways were to make circles to avoid crossing all but small rivers, the great expense and complicated engineering problems of making gigantic iron bridges must be faced.

VI

June and July

*

THE early months of 1848 had been months of gaiety, hope and even comedy. June was to be the month of tragedy and hate. Nothing is ever dead black; there were flashes of hope and signs of comfort. The German Assembly at Frankfurt at last took the step of appointing a supreme authority; it picked as Regent the Austrian Archduke John. He was a hard-working, amiable and competent man who had shown humane and almost democratic principles in the days of March in Vienna; the Prussian King naturally sulked at the news, but Austria would have sulked if a Prussian had been chosen, and both would have sulked if someone from a minor state had been elected. Indeed, the choice was probably a good one if the fundamental presumption of the Assembly had been true – that the various Emperors, Kings, Electors and Princes were ordinarily honest men and would keep their democratic promises. Anyway, the Regent picked a Cabinet and then there was, at last, an all-German government. Elsewhere there was muddle, but not disaster. The Slavs in the Austrian Empire were now in communication with each other – Bohemians angry at being made to speak German and Croats at being made to speak Latin or Magyar, and to these were added peoples called Slovaks, Ruthenes and Slovenes, names now heard for the first time. They all met in conference in Prague this month, with Poles from

Galicia and even some Serbs from Servia, and it was for a while doubtful if they were more hostile to the newly freed Austrians and Hungarians or to the old despotism of the Empire. The question was settled in favour of the first choice; the students from Prague University visited Vienna and there, as students will, quarrelled with the Viennese students. The battle was one of beer-mugs and speeches, more than anything else; but the influence of students was so disproportionate in both cities that the breach was fatal. Strangest of all, it survived actual civil war in Prague; Prince Windischgrätz, sent there by the Emperor and at that distance given the free hand he had longed for, bombarded the city and crushed the Slav constitutionalist movement. But the Slavs still regarded the Austrian and Hungarian peoples as their enemies, and the Viennese students were blind enough to send a deputation of congratulation to the Prince.[133]

There was, or there may have been an abortive attempt at revolution this month, of which no one knew. Thomas Frost, or whatever was his name, was warned some days beforehand by a member of the Chartist committee in London that the date for the armed uprising was Whit-Monday; it would be started from two centres, Blackheath south of the river and Bishop Bonners' Fields north of it, where meetings would be held. These meetings had been forbidden, but, said the Committeeman (whose name was Rose), they would be held anyway. On a second visit to his house in Croydon, south of London, Rose told Frost that warrants were out for every member of the committee, and there would therefore be only one assembly-place, Bishop Bonners' Fields, an open space in the City which has now vanished. Frost's duty on that day, with the rest of the Croydon

Chartists, was to hold meetings and demonstrate incessantly, so that all the local police would be pinned down in the borough and could not rush to the rescue of Westminster. This they did loyally on the Monday; although it rained all day the police force was kept on the run and not a single man could have gone up to London; but when evening came there was no news of a revolution and they went to bed disappointed. There is no direct account of what had happened in London; the story has to be pieced together from the newspapers. Some warning may have got through to the City police; anyway, they were in occupation of the Fields from early in the morning. Rain fell without ceasing, and as the Chartist contingents arrived they hesitated to try to force a way into the Fields, separately and without orders. They stood in the streets, the rain soaking them, until Dr. McDouall arrived; he made an attempt to get the police out of the way peacefully, but failed. Then he tried to find the committee-men and change the rendezvous to Lincoln's Inn Fields, but organization was bad, and he could not reach them. Besides, nothing would stop the rain; the Chartists were ill-clad, and any guns or pistols they may have had must have been useless by now. McDouall decided to dismiss them, and fight two months hence, when organization would be better.[134]

Nobody outside the Chartist ranks appeared to have noticed that anything had happened, but if the sun had shone on that Whit-Monday a serious attempt at revolution would clearly have been made. It could not have had any final success, no doubt; but it might have had a temporary one. There is evidence[135] of arming and drilling in the provinces sufficient to have pinned down forces elsewhere as the Croydon police were held.

Even their opponents admitted that the Chartists had more than 10,000 men in London who marched in formation and some at least of whom were armed; they themselves believed they had many more and they would have been correspondingly daring. On the other side the specials had gone home and the Duke's garrisons were back in barracks all round the Home Counties. A British Republic might have been proclaimed and have held Whitehall and part of London; if it had done so for merely a day even that would have influenced later British history – in what way, one can only speculate.

But what happened in London, Frankfurt or Prague did not matter this month; the tragedy which was the turning point of the year took place in Paris. Here there were two great forces moving towards a collision, with the senseless heaviness of two boulders falling against each other. The National Assembly, according to the Marxist interpretation which has later commanded most assent, represented the bourgeoisie, the Red Republicans of Paris the working class. At the time, the rival view was held that the conflict was one of the provinces against the capital or, more carefully phrased, of the countryman against the townsman. In any case, the assemblymen had recently been insulted, turned out of the Chamber, and even assaulted by the Parisian workers on a frivolous pretext. They naturally resented this, and reasonably regarded themselves as the representatives of the nation as a whole, who must be protected from any such bullying by a minority. But behind this determination to break the power of those who had invaded it, was another one, in the mind of a majority of the Assembly – to stop the apparently unending stream of francs which went out into the pockets of the unemployed, to annul the 'right to work' which had so lightly been approved in February, and to return to the system of uncontrolled private enterprise. For months trade had remained stagnant; this fact was to it a sufficient argument for the ending of the economic experiments of the revolution. To the working class of Paris, on the other side, it meant merely that the three months of poverty which it had made a present of to the Republic had been wasted. At the end, the proletarian was as hungry and miserable as ever. 'Labour' had not been 'organized'; the plan of Louis Blanc had been rejected and nothing else was offered. What should have been done, the Parisian worker might have found it hard to say, but he felt that he had been cheated. When the clash came, and Arago, the senior member of the Government, tried to reason with workers in the Rue Soufflot, they cried to him: 'You were with us in 1832! Don't you remember? – you built barricades with us then!'

'But not against the nation.'

'Monsieur Arago, you must not reproach us. You don't know what poverty is. You've never been hungry.'[136]

They had, indeed, little more than that to say – that they were hungry, and they ought not to be. They were not prepared to attack the Assembly, but they suspected an attack might be made on them at any time, and if so they were going to fight.

Yet a conflict was not inevitable; it was only made so by the character of the chief actors, or their lack of character. These were not the same people as had been at the front of the stage in February.

The most remarkable newcomer was one who had

tried to come forward then, had been told by Lamartine to go away at once, had done so within a few hours, and was still living in London. Prince Louis Napoleon Bonaparte was a small, skinny man at this date. He grew fatter later, but he never lost his yellow complexion, and his bloodshot and narrow eyes. He had a fuller moustache than Hitler's and a small tuft of a beard. Since he had retreated obediently in February he had hardly been heard of, and the politicians had discounted him. Suddenly his name reappeared. Half a dozen journals, priced at a halfpenny (5 centimes) or given away, medals with his profile on them, ribbons, little metal eagles, flags for the lapel, match-boxes with his picture upon them – where he got the money for all these historians still discuss, for he had been seedy and poverty-stricken enough a few weeks before. He was (he said) a 'working-class candidate'; he was in favour of the organization of labour and had written a book on the 'extinction of poverty'; he was even in favour of action on behalf of Poland.[137] He vociferated again and again his Republicanism. 'I will never ask for more rights than those of a French citizen. Nothing is changed in France; there is only one more Republican.'[138] (But he had already quite determined to kill the Republic; in a year remarkable for royal perfidy he has a pre-eminence of his own.)[139] He even tried anti-Semitism: 'Down with the Jews and the speculator Rothschild', but in the year 1848 it did not 'take' and he abandoned it. On June 4th there were supplementary elections to the Assembly, and to the astonishment of the Government he was elected in four different constituencies. There was an anxious debate. Should he be allowed to take his seat? The Bourbon pretenders, both of them, were excluded.

Shouldn't the Bonapartist be kept out too? The Assembly, swayed for the last time by Louis Blanc, decided to be generous and let him in. But he was more artful than they knew; he declined to take his seat, in a dignified letter which also contained a silky phrase to the effect that if in the future the people called on him he would do his duty.

No greater contrast to this rather reptilian figure can easily be imagined than the Archbishop of Paris. 'Saintly' applied to archbishops is usually as expected and meaningless a word as 'gracious' applied to kings; for Monseigneur Affre it was not wholly unjustified. Certainly some calculation entered in to his policy, but a saint is not necessarily silly. The Roman Church, or at least its French branch, had, like others, been meditating on the first revolution and was determined not to make the same mistakes in the second. The worst mistake was to have collided with the revolution head-on, and forced it into atheism. Affre and his clergy had therefore accepted the Republic this time and even encouraged it. They had helped to plant Trees of Liberty in February; they had tramped in in their great boots and black cloaks to bless every innocuous meeting, procession or dedication that they could; they had reminded the rich of their duty to the poor; there was even an eccentric *abbé*, named Lamennais, among the extreme 'red' deputies. The Vatican had not stopped them; the French Church was more independent-minded a century ago, and in any case Pius IX was in no state of mind to dictate a social policy to anyone. Affre saw the widening gap between the two ranks of society with fear and anxiety; he had determined to do all that lay in his limited power to force it to close again.

The man who was chiefly to frustrate him was, in his own way, as honest a man as he, and as single-minded. But that was all that could be said in favour of Eugene Cavaignac, who had recently become Minister of War. France more than most nations has suffered from the

GENERAL CAVAIGNAC, FROM A NEW PORTRAIT BY MARTINET.

brothers of great men. Because a Leclerc de Haute-cloque had a glorious record in the second world war, his brother was allowed to wreck Tunisia. Because Napoleon was a great general, a platoon of his brothers misruled half the states of Europe. Eugene Cavaignac was in the War Office at this crucial moment only because his brother Godefroy had been a man whose Republican nobility of character was a warm memory to every politician. He himself was a man without imagination or heart – rather stupid, rather cruel, technically competent, ambitious, but dull. He was a Republican by conviction; that is to say, he considered that the form of government called a republic was a better machine than any other. He was a type which was to be as common and influential in France up till 1939 as was the Anglo-Indian in England. That is, he was an officer who had fought in Africa. Of liberty, fraternity, the organization of labour, unemployment and so forth, he knew, and cared, nothing. All he knew was how to subdue natives.

There was nobody in the Government who could control him. Indeed, there was no government at all in any satisfactory sense of the word. Dupont (de l'Eure) had at last retired, and his great age had even before that made him little more than a figurehead anyway. François Arago, next in age, was an astronomer, and notably unfitted, as scientists usually are, for politics. Every other minister went his own way, and ill-luck had it that the key position was occupied by one of the pettiest, a man called Marie. He was Minister of Public Works, and had been responsible for the ill-run National Workshops from the beginning. His round, thin-whiskered face, with its little eyes and pursed-forward mouth, to some degree suggested his bureaucratic and legalistic mind. The National Workshops in his view were to be a semi-military organization which could be used to put down Louis Blanc's adherents – whether any work was done in them didn't matter, and this he had told his shocked chief administrator in the crudest terms.[140] Now, since M. Blanc had been disposed of, the National Workshops could be closed down. The administrator, in horror, told him this would mean civil war; Marie's reaction was to spend the next month arranging for the administrator to be eased out of his job and for another minister to have the technical responsibility for closing the workshops. The order was put out on June 21st, but with what seemed to him administrative cunning did not in so many words close the workshops.[141] That was not done till four days later. This decree compelled all workers between eighteen and twenty-five to join the army, expelled from Paris all other workers who could not 'formally prove residence' there for six months before May 24th, expelled any worker who did not take any job (whatever it might be) offered him by a private employer, stopped all current work in the shops while putting the payment of all who remained on the lists on piecework, and organized brigades to go out to drain the Sologne marshes, believed to be a malarial and dangerous job. Not a single workman could be deceived by this for more than a minute; it was like a cannon-shot. The workers in the shops were astounded, and crowded to the Luxembourg to protest the next morning. Their delegates were chosen almost by hazard; the one who spoke for them was named Louis Pujol. Marie hissed at him with the vehemence of a weak man: 'If the workers don't obey, we shall compel them by force. Do you hear? By force.'

'By force,' said Pujol. 'Very well. That tells us what we wanted to know.'

'And what did you want to know?'

'That the Government never has sincerely intended the organization of labour. Goodbye, citizen.'[142]

The Parisian workers were now an army without chiefs. They had subalterns, but no generals. The organization of the National Workshops was half-military; the foremen were named 'brigadiers', and the sections would move with perfect discipline. But all the possible leaders had been put into Vincennes prison after the uproar on May 15th. The Bonapartists tried their best to take their place; they set up cries of ''Poléon, 'Poléon,' and invented a sort of stamping slogan imitated by their successors ninety years later: 'NOUS-L'AUR-ONS; NOUS-L'AUR-ONS' (We will have him, we will have him). But they were too few, as yet, to have any effect; they had begun their campaign too late. Pujol, who had spoken to Marie, and summoned the workers to a mass meeting that evening, was to some small extent a leader, and one whose oddness is an indication of the lack of candidates. His sole publication was an apocalyptic pamphlet which read much more as if it had been written by an American or English evangelist than a Frenchman:

> Behold wherefore I prophesy unto you that the time to come hideth many bloody mysteries.
> Woe unto you who walk blindfold! Ye see not the abyss that shall swallow you.
> 'Verily I say unto you: All crimes will receive their punishment.'

Later he publicized and practised very advanced and somewhat shocking views on education and died in the service of the North in the American Civil War,[143] but that he was a commander or even a local leader of the Paris workers after the first day seems improbable; or indeed that anyone was.

A second meeting was held at six in the morning next day, Friday 23rd, by the Pantheon, and Pujol led it in procession to the Place of the Bastille, where everyone knelt before the column commemorating the prison's fall, and repeated after him the words 'Liberty or Death'.

Then they separated, and within a few minutes, after three blasts on a whistle, the first barricade was set up in the Rue St. Denis. It was manned, if that is the word, by between fifty and sixty women, and at the top was a tricolour flag with the inscription: 'National Workshops, 4th arrondissement, section 5.' Other barricades went up pretty steadily throughout the day; they

PARIS in 1848

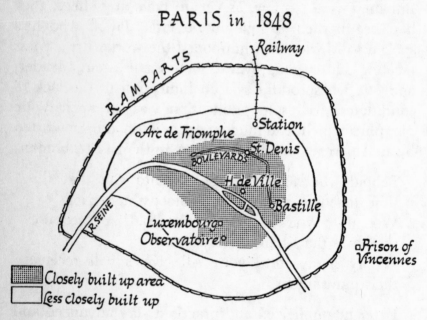

Closely built up area
Less closely built up

were solidly built and their defenders well drilled, but they did not seem to be located in accordance with any general plan, although each individual one was formidable.[144]

The Paris of 1848 was very different from the Paris of today. From the river northwards up to the Grands Boulevards – Capucines, St. Martin, and so on, where the showy shops and cafés now are – there was a closely knit mass of houses and small workshops, populated as thickly as any place in Europe. Between these boulevards and the outer boulevards – Rochechouart, La Villette, and so forth, narrower then and called *barrières* – were more houses and workshops, less closely set together. Then came a belt which was only half built up, where there were market gardens and open spaces, until one came to the great circle of the ramparts, whose site is now occupied by the long boulevards named after Napoleon's marshals, but which then were genuine military works. Beyond was open country. The southern bank of the river was similarly half-empty.

None of the great transverse streets that we know now pierced the central and important areas. The Boulevards Strasbourg, Sebastopol, Haussman, St. Germain, St. Michel, Magenta and Malesherbes and the Avenue de l'Opera did not exist; they were indeed only made because of the events of this week. The network of narrow streets had changed very little since the middle ages; they were narrowest, most knotted, and most difficult to penetrate round the Hôtel de Ville. The Hôtel de Ville itself was occupied by Government forces, but it was soon isolated, though the insurrectionaries, for some reason, made no concerted attack on it. Apart from it, however, most of the east of Paris was by nightfall covered with barricades. Draw a line from where now is the Gare du Nord southwards to the Observatoire; all east of it was in revolt.

The barricades went up slowly; most of them could have been stopped by quick and skilful action. The Government implored the Minister of War to move; General Cavaignac refused. 'If one of my platoons were disarmed, I should blow my brains out. Your shopkeepers can defend their shops themselves.' He meant by this the National Guard, which had indeed been called out, but a good proportion of which was sympathetic with the insurrection and moved listlessly; moreover, as Cavaignac knew well, it had not the guns to batter down the barricades. He had in fact his own plan; several of the assemblymen from the provinces were privy to at least part of it. It was to withdraw deliberately and let the insurrection come to a head. By this means the more courageous and intelligent of the rebels would have distinguished themselves and could be killed off; as for the mass of the population, it could be terrorized by a big slaughter. That was the way to deal with natives. During the process, it was only reasonable to hope, the Government would have been forced to resign and the General in charge would have taken over the executive power.[145]

Therefore, during the Friday, he deliberately only allowed dashes to be made at one barricade after another – enough to inflame the insurrection, to keep it confined (at least, to the extent that it did not actually invade the Assembly) and to lose the lives of a number of National Guards. Members of that body, which he considered undisciplined, could be spared, and he also had two other forces – the regular troops and the 'Garde Mobile'. M. Marie, who had thought he could rely on the National Workshops, had been uncertain of the Mobile Guard; he was wrong again. It was a new body; it had been recruited since February from families who were out of work and desperate. It consisted of boys from sixteen upwards, all of them young, tough, pale-faced and ill-grown; typical specimens from the Paris slums and half-slums. They would surely not (thought both M. Marie and the men of the National Workshops) shoot people who were their one-time friends and even in many cases their families, often actually their fathers. But they would; today's world which knows more about teen-age gangs is less surprised than Paris was. The boys had been well-fed for the first time in their lives, and given uniforms; now there was an opportunity to use revolvers and knives, and they did so. Besides, there were other attractions: plenty of spirits, free, and the praise and affection not just of girls, but (as soon as the going got tough) of real ladies. The Conservative press itself had to denounce as excessive the kissing and cuddling that went on in some places.

On Saturday all was ready. The insurgents had gained strength enough and had in fact been casting bullets all night; the battle was noisy and obviously serious; the Assembly was frightened and the Government had been forced to resign. Cavaignac had the power he wanted and now made a serious three-pronged attack on the rebels, directed by three generals who, like him, had served in Algeria. One column, on the extreme north, started pushing along south of Montmartre towards La Villette. In the centre, an attack was made straight towards the Hôtel de Ville; the insurgents had got 'within sixty paces' of it before it was freed. In the south progress was swifter; the Left Bank seemed cleared, and Herzen, a Russian refugee, that evening passed groups of Mobile Guards who were celebrating, surrounded by admiring women. One boy kept boasting that he had bayoneted six insurgents in the stomach; he was very drunk.

The next day was Trinity Sunday; the date meant nothing to either side. There begun for the first time – the year is rich in commencements, of evil and of good – a skilfully organized atrocity campaign: 22,000 convicts,

it was said, had been released to join the insurrection.
The barricades were decorated with the heads of
prisoners shot after capture. All the women in the
convents in Eastern Paris had been raped and shot.
A Socialist corpse had been found with a ticket in its
pocket entitling the bearer to 'three ladies from the
Faubourg St. Germain'. The insurgents were supplying
the soldiers with poisoned cigars. (The British Ambassador credited this last one, and noted it in his
memoirs.) If the insurgents believed similar nonsense
it will never be known; all that they left behind was a
few inscriptions, 'Work or Death!', 'Peace and Freedom',
'Social Justice', and a couple of posters asking for the
right to work.[146] But they had put back a number of the
destroyed barricades, especially on the Left Bank, and
they had even cast a huge cannon which women were
cooling by throwing water and sand on it. When
Cavaignac's columns attacked again at dawn, they found
that a good deal of the ground they thought they had
won was lost. The battle was bloody; trying to storm
those tall and solid barricades was not an easy job, but,
oddly enough, Cavaignac seemed to care very little for
casualties among the troops he had been so unwilling to
risk two days before. A general was captured and killed;
others were seriously wounded. By late afternoon,
however, the central column and the southern had
pushed along both banks of the Seine, and thereafter
joined each other by the Place of the Bastille, where
there was a barricade the height of three men in front of the
Column of July, from which the red flag was flying.
They did not take the barricade, but their junction
meant that rebel Paris was cut into two parts and the
insurrection now had no real chance of success. A

sort of hysteria had come over the troops by now, probably because of the atrocity stories. They were shooting their prisoners, or setting on them and kicking and beating them until they were seriously injured; the Mobile Guard and some National Guards who had been brought in from the provinces were worse than the regulars.

It was at this point that Archbishop Affre saw, or

THE GREAT BARRICADE AT THE ENTRANCE OF THE RUE DU FAUBOURG ST. ANTOINE, FROM THE PLACE DE LA BASTILLE.

thought he saw, his opportunity to stop the slaughter and perhaps out of the very horror of the disaster to revive a feeling of unity in society. He was strongly dissuaded by his Vicar-General and the other Palace officials when he told them what his plan was; he was only supported in it by a turbulent group of 'social-minded' young priests whom he had for years protected and encouraged. These latter induced him to change his plan in one respect; he was going out in ordinary clerical clothes, but they made him wear his violet robes and on his breast his great archbishop's cross.

He walked on foot to Cavaignac's headquarters and told him that he must be authorized to offer peace to the insurgents. The General must write a proclamation to that effect; the attack must stop; he, the archbishop, would in person carry it to the barricades. Cavaignac was very unwilling; but in face of Affre's almost majestic determination he gave way. He wrote a proclamation in warm terms, ending 'The arms of the Republic are open to receive you'; the priest approved it and started on his mission.

He walked with a few attendants as far as the Place of the Arsenal, blessing ambulances and soldiers as he passed and, by all accounts, quietening or dissipating the hysteria around him. At this point he came into the danger zone; after a consultation, a short cortège was formed, all of civilians, the archbishop in the second rank, preceded by a man holding a branch broken from an olive tree. They walked through narrow streets where there was only casual firing, which was stilled from the Government side as they passed. As they left the Rue de l'Orne they came in sight of the huge barricade at the Place de la Bastille, barring the way to the Faubourg St. Antoine. The Colonel in command of the troops ordered a cease-fire, with a roll of drums; the insurgents respected the conventional signal and there was a sudden and complete silence. The archbishop and his colleagues, joined by an Assemblyman, walked slowly across the empty square to the foot of the barricade. A single rebel made a derisive remark; no one else spoke.

One of his cortège, by name Ricard, clambered on to

the barricade and began to read the proclamation: 'I exhort you in the name of all that is sacred, lay down your arms! The whole nation asks this of you. . . .' He pointed to the archbishop standing below. 'Look. His Grace the Archbishop has come among you, to stop the killing of his children.' There was hardly any hesitation; the rebels were all round him, shaking his hand, patting his shoulder and clambering down to get the archbishop's blessing. They begged the priest to come through the barricade; in this battle, they said, he should be the one that was victorious. Let the proclamation be read on every barricade, they cried, pointing down the Faubourg St. Antoine, where there was barrier after barrier. Some of them ran out into the square; others helped up the archbishop, who turned his face toward the Faubourg. The man with the green bough stood by him, waving it so that the next barricade could see.

Just what happened next is uncertain, but it appears that quarrels broke out in the square between the soldiers and the rebels; some of the Mobile Guards tried to seize the workers' rifles and knock them about. A shot rang out, and then a full volley. The archbishop stood up in full prominence, with hands and voice trying to stop it. 'Friends, friends,' he kept crying, until a bullet struck him in the spine and he fell into the arms of the man with the green bough, which dropped on to the ground. Who fired the shot will never be known; it was probably an accident, but it seems clear that it came from the Government side.[147] Naturally, perhaps, the story was put about that the rebels had deliberately shot Affre, though in fact they were tending him with frenzied anxiety. When the doctor told him that his wound was mortal, he said: 'May God grant, then, that my blood is the last to be spilled.' But his prayer was not heard; the war had restarted.

The next day's fighting was the same in kind as Sunday's. There were some attempts at negotiation, but Cavaignac would accept 'nothing but victory'. The barricades were taken one by one, at great expense, but with lessening loss of life as they were turned by columns coming from their rear. By the end of the day, all resistance was over. What then followed was not a new thing, but a revival; the massacre of the helpless. 'A volume could be filled with accounts of the atrocious scenes; there was shooting everywhere, in the streets, the cemeteries, the quarries of Montmartre and Butte Chaumont.' The historian who writes this[148] estimates that 3,000 were killed after the fighting was over, deliberately. Some were killed in the temporary prisons – the gardens of the Luxembourg, the subterranean rooms at the Tuileries, and the cellars of public buildings. Some soldiers – not usually the regulars – shot through the ventilators into the mass of prisoners, as a sort of amusement. 'Duck-shooting' they called it. In one cellar the prisoners begged for bread; it was an officer who answered them with a smile: 'Wait a moment.' He took a rifle from a private and fired through the ventilator. A prisoner fell. 'Is anyone else hungry?' said the officer. 'Can I serve any gentleman?'[149]

The silence that followed this deadly week-end seemed in a sense to spread all over Europe. Comment was hushed; the nations were horrified, but none of them as yet knew what to think or what would result. Nor could they, nor indeed can we; for the results of those four dreadful days are not yet over. They have

been especially long-lasting in France; that nation has
ever since been divided into two, the one section haunted
by fear and guilt, the other by hatred and a desire for
revenge. The Paris Commune, twenty-three years
later, was nothing but a repetition of the days of June,
on a vaster scale, crueller yet, and lasting for two months.
The French *bourgeois* and *proletaire*, by a tradition starting
in June and since then passed from father to son, have
each believed that the other would kill him if the chance
came, and that behind the large speeches of politicians
was a reality of class war and death which should never
be forgotten. In 1940, when the Nazi threat drove all
British classes together into one unit, the French nation
fell apart; the Army held back forces to deal with the
'reds' at home, Stalinists fawned round the German
headquarters; to this day the two classes do not speak the
same language.

There were two young theorists who were in no way
surprised – or so they claimed – by the 'June Days'.
Marx and Engels had written their famous *Communist
Manifesto* at the end of 1847 for a small international
Socialist League; it had been published without attract-
ing much interest; but now it seemed to them, and has
seemed to many people since, that its thesis had been
proved within a few weeks of its appearance. They had
the prestige of prophets whose prophecies are fulfilled
within a month or two, while the public still remembers
them. Nor is it possible even now to reject their interpretation; historians who do are reduced to such petu-
lant or frivolous explanations as blaming the failures of
1848 on 'the Jews' or 'the intellectuals' or some other
scapegoat.[150] Up till now (they argued in broad terms)
revolutions had been bourgeois revolutions – that is to

say, the revolution had been led by members of the middle class and had had for its objects those rights most necessary for a middle-class society – freedom of the person, freedom of trade, the abolition of feudal laws and relationships, and in general the end of the rule of royalty and the landed aristocracy. This type of revolution, so led and so manned, was now being overtaken by another kind of revolution. The development of capitalist society, which provided the real strength behind the revolution of 1789 and the first revolution of 1848, had ineluctably led to the appearance of another class, the great class of the property-less workers. This class could only succeed by turning out the *bourgeoisie*, just as the latter was turning out the nobility. Therefore, as soon as a revolution had commenced, the *bourgeoisie* would be paralysed by the appearance behind it, like a spectre, of the working class which wanted to seize its property and inaugurate a Communist state. That was what had happened in June. The *bourgeoisie* had gaily started in February with the old slogans; in June it had had to face the demand of the workers to take over its property and form a classless society. In the future, the same thing would always happen. The role of the *bourgeoisie* as a progressive force was over; it was now conservative. Also (they added) it was doomed.

The years to come underlined the truth of what they said. Among the more pathetic documents of history is a 'Manifesto of the Republican Party'[151] issued in 1855 and signed by Mazzini, Kossuth and Ledru Rollin, the three names that once would have moved more millions than any others. 'Insurrection,' it concludes, 'will engender insurrection, and the first victory ten others at ten different points. There is not a nation which may not by an energetic and powerful act of will be the cause of the salvation of the world.' Absolute silence greeted it; it is a sheet in the gutter of history, picked up by the curious. None of those to whom they appealed answered. To find support for any revolutionary change, or even for any important reform, a politician henceforward had to turn to the East Ends of the great towns, to coalfields, ship-yards, cotton mills and iron foundries. Their programmes had to be what the mill-hands and miners wished to hear; they had to be programmes of social equality.

The flaw in the Marxist interpretation was that (in accordance with the metaphysical fantasy called Dialectical Materialism) it assumed that an event could have only one cause. It must be the Antithesis of a Thesis (or a Negation of an Affirmation – the pseudo-Hegelian phrases varied) and would be itself transmuted into a Synthesis (or a Negation of the Negation) which would combine the qualities of both Thesis and Antithesis. No one but a German philosophical student would have expected such a formula to work, and in fact the decline in the fortunes of the revolutionaries which set in immediately after June had, outside of France, several causes. Among them the 'revolt of the proletariat' was very small – indeed, generally non-existent, except in so far as alarm and depression at the news from Paris made men of all classes less unwilling to accept the reappearance of Kings and Emperors. What choked the revolutionaries from July onwards was their own follies, and these follies proceeded mostly from a cause not allowed for in the Marxist analysis. It was the natural vice of nationalism. Until now, it had been presumed without proof, as the three signatories continued to presume until their deaths, that each freed nation would respect the freedom of every other freed nation, and that the world would thus automatically become a peaceful federation of Young Ireland, Young Italy, Young Austria, Young Hungary and so forth. In the days when 'the nation' had first been exalted by the French revolution, that assumption had been natural and not necessarily absurd. For devotion to the nation then meant devotion to the common good, to the republic, as opposed to serving a king or an aristocracy; it was a formula for internal regeneration. But once that first phase was past, nationalism became a glorification of one's own nation as opposed to others'. It became no more respectable or enlightened than the assertion that one's own family is better than next-door's; and, like that snobbish vanity, easily and perhaps inevitably turned into quarrelsomeness. The student squabbles of Vienna and Prague were repeated all over Europe; they could not be composed because the squabblers believed they had right and history on their side. The chief beneficiary was the Austrian Emperor, for his Court had always believed that any race could be set to fight another, and that that was the first recipe for keeping the Hapsburgs indefinitely in power. (The second was to marry the right princesses.)[152]

The immediate dividend came in Italy. The freed Hungarians were willing that Hungarian regiments should be used against Italians. The Croats and Czechs were willing to fight for the Emperor anywhere, though on the whole they would have preferred to fight Hungarians. Marshal Radetzky, therefore, with these extra forces was able to reconstruct his army and prepare a plan of campaign. King Charles Albert of Piedmont, on the other hand, was still playing politics – successfully enough. The Venetian Republic by July 4th understood the alternative put before it – apply to be annexed by Charles Albert or be left to the Austrian army. Its Assembly voted gloomily for the first choice and sent a rather synthetic address of loyalty to Piedmont. Charles Albert was now King of all North Italy.

His reign lasted three weeks. Radetzky moved in to attack, and a mystical and crafty king proved no match for an eighty-year-old professional. The Piedmontese troops fought bravely enough when the clash came at Custozza on the 27th, but by the end of the day it was clear Charles Albert had not just lost a battle; he had lost a war. He fled with his wrecked army back to Piedmont, abandoning Milan and all Lombardy; the Venetians, with some relief mingling with their alarm, cancelled their vote of July 4th and retired behind their lagoons, once again as the 'Republic of St. Mark'. The Duke of Genoa, Charles Albert's son, decided that this was not a time to accept the offer from the local revolutionaries to become King of Sicily.

The end of the Irish revolution was less bloody, but also less inspiring. Nothing had happened when Mitchel, their best orator, had been sentenced in May, and in the dream world of the Young Irelanders this was the final shame which all Ireland would rise to wipe out. Overpersuaded, or perhaps himself deluded, Smith O'Brien the M.P. led an insurrection in July. The British authorities took it seriously enough to issue posters offering rewards for the arrest of the generals and describing them vividly if not complimentarily:

William Smith O'Brien, sallow long face, has a sneering smile constantly, well-set man, walks erect, dresses well . . . *John Dillon*, dark hair, dark eyes, thin sallow face, rather thin black whiskers; dressed respectable; has bilious look. . . . *Michael Doheny*, sandy hair, grey eyes, coarse red face like a man given to drink, high cheek bones, wants several of his teeth, very vulgar appearance, small short red

ARREST OF SMITH O'BRIEN AT THE RAILWAY STATION AT THURLES.

whiskers. . . . *T. D. Reilly*, five feet seven inches in height, round freckled face, head remarkably broad at the top, broad shoulders; well set; dresses well. . . .

But the country was exhausted and indifferent; no phalanxes of volunteers rose to their call. There was only one battle, which is known in history, correctly enough, as the battle of the Cabbage Patch. Near

Ballingarry in Tipperary the Young Irelanders attacked about sixty armed policemen, who retreated into a stout and square cottage owned by Mrs. Cormack, a widow. The rebels tried to take it, approaching through the widow's cabbage patch and shooting rather uselessly at the little windows of the house. They were exposed to more effective rifle fire – cabbages give but little cover – and though it is not sure that any of them were killed several were wounded and it was fairly soon clear that their attempt was hopeless. The rebel army retreated and broke up. Smith O'Brien, deserted by his followers, was arrested when trying in Thurles railway station to buy a second-class ticket to Limerick. The three next in command gave themselves up one night to some police-men who were standing at a cross roads near Rath-common. Death sentences were pronounced, none of which were carried out. All were changed to deportation which itself was soon after commuted. Smith O'Brien ended his life comfortably enough in a country house in Wales. Mitchel became an advocate of slavery in the Southern States of America; others of the Young Irelanders became ministers or members of Parliament in Australia and Canada.

A tide that is ebbing in the wide bays of the ocean may appear to be rising still in distant creeks and long inlets. The news of February had taken a long time to reach the consciousness of the people of the West Indies; the steamship *Dee*, which left the West Indies on July 15th, brought an account of the first and only movement by a race which had never yet – or only once – taken liberty for itself. The Danish King ruled three small islands in the Caribbean, St. Thomas, St. Croix and St. John; the Negroes there were still slaves. The Negroes of

St. Croix (why there, and not in the other islands, is not recorded) decided that King Frederick's new democratic constitution ought to apply to them too; they rose in a well-organized revolt. The island is small and there were not many whites to resist them; the governor, Herr Scholten, is said too to have been a timorous man. It was also charged that the merchants and planters who lived in St. Croix had been oppressive in their conduct, in particular by exercising a sort of *droit de seigneur* over the young and pretty black girls, or merely by keeping harems. Herr Scholten announced that the Danish Parliament had agreed to free all slaves, over a period of twelve years and in return for complicated payments; the concession was too late. The Negroes captured the two small settlements of Christianstad and Frederikstad, the only towns on the island; Governor Scholten pleading with them to 'pillage only a little', and not to imitate the whites in their behaviour to women. He also declared slavery abolished at once. The merchants and their families, in fact, had escaped on board three ships in the harbour, one Danish and two English. Here they held a meeting which deposed Governor Scholten and decided to fetch in Spanish troops from Porto Rico; with these troops they counter-attacked and re-took the island. But though the Negroes were put down, and a new Danish Governor was installed, the real victory was with the blacks. Slavery was abolished and stayed abolished. The Danish colonies joined the British and French as islands of freedom, under the lee of the vast slave-market of Cuba and the even vaster southern states of the American Union. Only armed force, and white armed force at that, could free the Negroes there; but Lord George Bentinck was not going to be able to arrange the invasion of Cuba, nor was anyone seriously considering an attack on the Southern States, except brooding John Brown in Springfield.[153] Jefferson Davis, not as yet a very distinguished politician, said in the Senate that he would as soon fear an insurrection from his cows as from his slaves.[154]

VII

August

*

AUGUST and the first week of September used to be
called the Silly Season. It was assumed that no
news of any importance would be received then,
and that the press could safely concentrate on frivolous
items. It was the time for sea-serpents, giant marrows,
one-eyed tribes in Central Africa, and voyages to the
moon. Not until this period had been chosen to start
two world wars in was the belief abandoned. It was
true enough in 1848. There certainly was one revolution (the year demanded it), but it was in the fairy-tale
land of Persia, and the details which were reported had a
pantomime character. The Armenians of Tabriz had
been abducting girls from harems; the Moslems of
Tabriz turned on them and drove them out of the city;
they also expelled the Government officials, who had
been privy to the Armenian naughtinesses. An authority
called the Salar of Khorassan defeated the whole Persian
army. The Shah insulted the Russian Ambassador, who
walked out of the Palace uttering dreadful threats.
Another Shah called Nasruddin had taken his place.[155]

There was a war as well as a revolution, but it was a
distant war, and reports were gratifying and entertaining. The difficulties of General Gough, the sixty-eight-
year-old British Commander in the Punjab, were
similar to those facing Sir Harry Smith in South Africa,
increased by his having behind him a Governor-General

of thirty-seven, Lord Dalhousie, who was as bumptious
and melodramatic as Sir Harry without his background
of experience. In India as in South Africa, Parliamentary opposition to imperialism prevented any system-
atic scheme of conquests; it was necessary instead to
surround British possessions with a ring of reliable native
states, with whose rulers one could live in peace. But,
though there were fortunately no slave-minded Dutch-
men to complicate the problem, the Indian rajahs were
no more reliable than the Kaffir chiefs; their promises of
peaceful behaviour were equally promptly broken. Two
English officers had been murdered in April in the
Punjab, by the treachery of the Mulraj, the most
important Sikh leader. The 'Durbar' in Lahore, a sort
of board which was supposed to be the main Sikh government, pretended to be still in alliance with the British;
it even provided a column of troops headed by a general
called Shere Singh to assist in punishing the Mulraj.
By manœuvring in concert with Shere Singh, General
Gough had been driving the Mulraj into the fortress of
Multan; he caught up with him near to his camp at
Buggerahrah, and there inflicted on his army a severe
defeat, capturing six guns and all his baggage. The
victory does not appear in the history books; whether
from its inelegant name or because it was not so important as the reporters thought, but anyhow it enabled
the British to advance right to the walls of Multan, which
were vehemently and noisily defended by 'guns, jingals,
zumbooruks, bows and arrows, etc.',[156] whatever they
might be. All seemed well to the Governor-General;
General Gough was less at ease.

Sir Harry's victory also came this month, and if it,
too, was not as final as he believed he at least could

have had no reason to suspect so. Pretorius, the Boer farmer whom he had trusted, had turned against him. He had crossed the River Vaal, beyond British territory, to a settlement called Magalisberg, which he made a rallying point for Dutch farmers who resented the British policy towards the blacks, and were determined that South African society should be one of white supremacy over Kaffir labourers. Their principles and their habits of life were derived from the Old Testament, the only book which they read; they were as merciless and as visionary as John Brown, but their vision was the opposite of his. Towards the end of July Pretorius felt he had collected enough of them to form a force which was given the then odd name of a Commando, and with them he recrossed the Vaal with the intention of conquering what is now the Orange Free State. He did so; he reached Bloem-fontein, and expelled the representatives of the Queen, telling them to go back to Capetown. Sir Harry Smith had been caught unprepared by this audacity, and it took a week or two to collect enough troops to deal with it. When he was ready, he marched north across the Orange River; Pretorius's force backed away from him; he re-entered Bloemfontein; eventually, the Boers made a stand on August 29th at a place called Boomplats, where there was a 'neck' between two hills which would give their riflemen an advantage. The battle was not very long, nor very severe. Nineteen English soldiers were killed and about nine Boers; the Dutch force broke up in defeat and the irreconcilables among them crossed the Vaal River to make what living they could in the almost empty veldt of the trans-Vaal country. Sir Harry did not bother to pursue them. The question, he may quite reasonably have thought, was now settled.

South Africa would be developed on the lines of enlightened Victorian liberalism; the slave-holding Dutch
were finished with and all that needed to be feared was a
recrudescence of Kaffir savagery. On that he may perhaps have begun to suspect the weak foundations of the
optimism of Mrs. Jenkins of Pondo Land and the other
missionaries. He could never have thought, nor did
anyone else, that in a century's time the descendants of
Pretorius's commando would be establishing all over
South Africa almost exactly the colour-bar oligarchy
which they had intended and he had prevented.[157]

The sensations of August otherwise were mostly
natural in origin, or at least if man-made were not
man-intended. A hurricane tore along the east side of
Scotland, from Aberdeen to Wick, picking up something like a thousand fishing boats in its course and
strewing the long coasts with wrecked ships and the bodies
of fishermen. An even worse one visited Antigua, St.
Kitt's and Nevis in the West Indies, tearing down the
buildings and uprooting plantations until 'neat islands of
populous villages' became 'wastes of rubbish'. More
appalling, because more concentrated, was the fate of
the *Ocean Monarch*, 'the most beautiful and splendid' of
the great number of American emigrant ships. She burst
into flames in the Irish Channel; 'in maddened despair
women jumped overboard with their offspring in their
arms and sank to rise no more'; rescuers could hardly
approach owing to the great heat; half the passengers
died; the ship itself burnt to the water's edge, when
'volumes of flame shot into the air with a hissing sound'
until the water 'at length buried this once noble vessel'.
Half Albany Street, near Regent's Park in London, was
destroyed by the modern invention of gas-light. A

dealer in Berlin wool there had closed and locked his shop, but late at night was awoken by a disgreeable smell, and went downstairs to search for its origin with a candle, as anyone would. When he opened the door to the shop there was a gigantic explosion; an escape of gas had turned the whole tightly-closed ground floor into a sort of monstrous box-bomb, which blew the house into the air and damaged a hundred others nearby. There was very little loss of life, but the damage was immense and the whole area was incommoded by the smell of flying and smouldering hanks of Berlin wool. There were many who drew the moral that new-fangled devices were dangerous; but they were refuted by news from a city where no new-fangled devices were allowed. 'Most of the principal buildings' of Constantinople were burnt down owing to a fire in the depot called Yagh Kapan, which contained oil for lamps. The arsenal was burnt, and the fire attacked the compact mass of small shipping moored near it. The spectacle was made 'more sublime' in the opinion of a rather callous observer by the reflection of the flames in the water, the 'shrill cries' of the captains, and the 'long, continuous and savage howls of the mariners' trying to sail away. The Mosque of Suleymanieh and the palaces of seven Pashas were burnt down.[158]

What happened in the East was, after all, expected to be fantastic; public opinion was rather more shocked by the burning of about a quarter of a much smaller town, Albany, the capital of New York State. This fire broke out August 17th in a stable; no adequate attempt was made to put it out, and a wind came roaring up from the south at almost gale strength. It blew the flames like waves of fire up Broadway to State Street; the wooden houses were so much fuel. Here, too, the ships and steamers in the river only just escaped by putting out towards New York; as it was, many persons leapt into the water to avoid the flames and so died. All the riverside area was ash; nearly a hundred canal boats were destroyed. The firemen were helpless or incompetent; the fire was only stopped by a steady downpour at evening and the blowing up of houses which were in its path.[159]

But disasters were far from being the typical news from the United States; on the contrary, the States were bounding forward. As Boston was preparing to challenge Manchester as a centre of morality, austere culture and enlightened economic policy, so New York could offer some rivalry to London in gaiety and sophistication. It had one social attraction, at least, that the Old Country could not offer. 'The Ice-Cream Saloons of Broadway', said the writer of *New York in Slices*,[160] 'are fitted up in a style of exaggerated finery. . . . At night the gaudy curtains, silver paper, and gilded mirrors are highly illuminated by Gaslight. . . . Every one is crowded with throngs of well dressed men and women.' The Irish, being less well dressed, patronized (one reads with slight surprise) 'the Confectionery Shops of the Bowery'. For 25 cents (children half-price) the New Yorkers could see a show that London certainly could not equal – the series of Sacred Dioramas. On 'a rich Gothic proscenium' the audience saw in the first part (whose curtain rose at eight o'clock) the whole of the Creation reproduced, day by day. The New York press, usually irreverent, treated it with awed respect – no wonder, for here is a description of one of the Days:

CREATION OF FISH AND FOWL – THE 5TH DAY

Morning again dawns upon the inanimate beauties of the creation; but, lo! the mighty monsters of the deep are seen moving through the trackless waters! The vast deep is teeming with life! The melodious warbling of birds strikes upon the ear! And there may be seen moving about, among the foliage, every variety of the feathered tribe; and the rising moon closes the Fifth Day.

Part Second was 'a continuous Diorama of the Deluge'. Many of the audience at this point found the tragedy unbearable. 'With upraised hands, the fugitives appear to supplicate for mercy! But it is too late! Their awful doom is sealed.'

Though 'mud was ankle deep in Fulton Street' in wet weather, 'and other streets not much better',[161] the city was making a bid to be a centre of fashion too. One of its hatters even had a rival to Regent Street's Idrotobolic hat. The already famous family of Beebe, (William H., New York and Philadelphia) presented this month 'an entirely new and unique Hat; surpassing any hat that has ever been produced'; it had the surprising quality of automatically 'adapting itself *particularly* to the size and features *of each individual wearer*'. Its makers, in offering this remarkable and chameleontic hat, remarked reasonably enough that 'nothing is more incongruous than the contrast between a *large face* and a *small hat*', and added provokingly that they would never sell a hat at as low a price as $4. No picture, once again, appears to have survived of this unusual product; it roused bitter jealousy and open derision in rival hatters, particularly from Mr. Knox, the price of whose hats was $4.[162]

Food was ample and fresh in the city, and was quoted in a curious mixture of old and new currencies. Apples in Washington market, N.Y.C., this August were $1 or $2 a barrel. Good sweet corn had fallen to fourteen ears for 1s.; cheese was 7 to 9 cents a pound. Chickens were 'fine' at 3s. 6d. or 4s. 6d. a pair; mutton 'is 6 to 10 cents a pound; it is very good – sweet and tender'. Eggs were eleven for 1s. retail; watermelons about 2s. Yellow-legged snipe were just coming in at 10s. a dozen; 'wild pigeons are gone'.[163]

A sea-serpent, naturally, was observed this month – in Vermont, rather surprisingly. How it got there was doubtful, but there was no doubt about its size; it was 'as large as a common stove-pipe' and about 12 feet long. 'He has a rather venomous look. His colour is a dark brown.'[164] But, really, it was not for the marvels of nature so much as the marvels of man's achievement that the United States was already remarkable. There was one by which even the coldest of English observers was moved to enthusiasm.

The Suspension Bridge at Niagara Falls is a most sublime work of art – it is impossible to give a clear idea of the grandeur of the work. Imagine a bridge 800 feet in length hung in the air, at the height of 230 feet, over a vast body of water rushing through a narrow gorge at the rate of thirty miles an hour. To a spectator below it looks like a strip of paper suspended by a cobweb. When the wind is strong, the frail gossamer-looking structure sways to and fro as if ready to start from its fastenings, and it shakes from extremity to centre at the firm tread of a pedestrian. But there is no danger – men pass over it with perfect safety while the head of the timid looker-on swims with apprehension.[165]

This marvellous achievement was marred by a conflict which would have distressed the European admirers of America if they had heard of it. The contractors who built the Bridge and the directors of the company quarrelled, making accusations of the grossest financial dishonesty against each other and even coming to blows – at least, to the extent that the directors seized by force the tolls taken from foot passengers at the Canadian end, and continued to do so throughout August.[166]

The picture which European Republicans had made for themselves of American life was, indeed, an unreal one; it was painted to suit their own needs and their own hopes, from materials drawn not from contemporary America but from the United States of Washington and Jefferson. Louis Blanc could never have suspected that the most influential and intelligent Boston periodical, the *North American Review*, was analysing his own programmes and his colleagues' characters in terms of sour contempt worse than Lord Normanby's, and for the same reason – that they had shown neglect of the rights of private property.[167] No European republican would have believed that republican politicians in America could receive, let alone have earned, the contempt in which some at least were already held. Almost any issue of the *Daily Tribune*, edited by Horace Greeley, the greatest and most enlightened of American journalists, contained paragraphs which they would have found literally incredible; here is one, from the issue of August 9th:

Stealings: The members of Congress have voted themselves the usual allowance of books all round – about six hundred dollars worth each, we believe. The cost to the Treasury is estimated at one hundred

and twenty thousand dollars: and the Members
might with equal propriety have voted themselves
a hogshead of Madeira each and a silver goblet to
drink it from. If they would only *read* the books
there would be some excuse for this swindle but nine
tenths of them will leave Congress as ignorant as
they entered it.

The members of the French Government which had
recently resigned left office poorer than they entered;
however deluded they may have been, the German and
Italian leaders were equally high-minded. They voted
themselves no expenses, no libraries. They would not, as
Senator Butler was reported as doing this month, attempt
to silence an opponent by forcing him to a murderous
duel.[168] Though they would perhaps have realized that
American campaign speeches were not of profound
importance they probably would have been disquieted by
the subjects which their distant heroes dilated upon, so
different from the idealistic if unpractical nature of their
own proposals. The candidates' speeches revolved in
particular far too much round the recent war upon
Mexico – Vera Cruz was only evacuated this month –
which was after all, a conflict in which a weaker republic
had had a large territory wrested from it by force. It
was, perhaps, only human nature that the victory should
be celebrated, and the Sacred Dioramas, at the end of
the month, should be outdone by a Mammoth Panor-
ama, on 406 Broadway, being nineteen thousand square
feet of painting showing the full details of General
Taylor's victories in Mexico. General Zachary Taylor,
a Whig, had formally accepted nomination for the
Presidency; apart from his victories, his claims, like

those of Louis Napoleon, were chiefly urged on personal and demagogic grounds. All could recognize him (said Representative Crittenden at Russellville, Kentucky) 'in his old brown coat as old ROUGH AND READY, as a real republican'. Old Zack would beat them all; no man could look five minutes into his face and then 'make a proposition of a mean action'.[169] But what his opponent,

Dennington's Floating Church for Seamen at Philadelphia

the Democratic General Cass, the slave-owners' friend, said was far worse. He did more than rejoice over the Mexican war; he wanted to repeat it and to carry on what later would have been called 'aggressive imperialist' wars in several other directions. 'Come on,' said his organ, the *True Sun*, 'come on, we say, Mexico, Cuba, Jamaica, Canada. The shield of the Union is broad enough for you all.' It was certainly believed and may have been true,[170] that Cass had a completed plan to re-invade Mexico on the 'spontaneous' appeal of what were flippantly called 'buffalo-hunters', organized and directed from New Orleans. The Havana correspondent of the *Picayune*, his organ in that city, sent despatches assuring the readers that all Cubans too, but more particularly the Creoles, were in the grip of a 'universal' longing for annexation by the United States. Greeley[171] was sufficiently disturbed by this campaign to examine the plan seriously. The United States, he said, could 'easily' conquer Canada among the proposed annexations, but could never acquire Cuba unless they were prepared to spend 'a hundred million dollars' on building a navy equal to the British.

The same excellent editor printed other information which European admirers would have regretted, but at least would have understood. Greeley sent the writer who had surveyed New York society for him down to Philadelphia to do the same. He found that this city's position, which had made it the natural refuge for escaping slaves from the south, had not raised its moral and social standards. Far from it; the freed coloured population was the most degenerate and vicious agglomeration of people that he had ever seen. It was not the Negroes' fault:

The largest collections of them reside in Lombard Street and its vicinity – being like all poor people in cities crammed into lofts, garrets and cellars, in blind alleys and narrow courts, with no sewerage, gas or water, with not a breath of pure fresh air from one week to another. They cannot help being horribly immoral and disgustingly filthy. One of the first lessons that the African has been taught by the white man is that chastity and marriage are a mockery, and consequently the social life of this degraded class is utterly beastly and beyond hope of redemption in this generation.

The females had but one occupation, prostitution. The male occupations were 'begging, working a little, and especially stealing'. But, concluded the writer, gentler and more far-seeing than most of his colleagues, anyone who looked at them closely could see in even the runaway slaves 'an innate capacity for self-improvement'.

It would not have been easy to find in the English daily press studies as important, as tolerant, or as well-written. The Silly Season was indeed silly; or, to be fairer, there was room for reporting incidents of an oddity, variety, or grotesquery typical of an old England which was already disappearing, quickly enough to be an object of curiosity. There was, for example, even in the modern city of Leeds the case of Benjamin Holmes, an hotel-keeper. He had made a habit of seducing women past their first youth, by the promise of marriage and an assured position. The Leeds ladies consulted, and arranged for one of their number, a widow, to indicate a probable compliance, and to invite him to tea, which would be laced with rum. While he was enjoying this mixture, the door was opened; the ladies' delegation entered; they poured over him some tar provided by the Leeds Gas Company; and shook the contents of a feather pillow over the tar.[172] They then chased him along the main street. A grimmer survival of Old England was seen later in the same week. Three dozen lashes were inflicted on a young man called Henry Killerby at Guildford for an attempt at poisoning.

'Public floggings are now very rare', observed *Lloyd's News* regretfully, and 200 people came to the spectacle.

The Archaeological Institute of Great Britain and Ireland, meeting in Lincolnshire, showed that eighteenth century methods of scientific and historical investigation survived unchanged. (The British Association, also meeting this month and attended by Dr. Faraday, conducted its proceedings very differently.) Its host society, the Gentlemen's Society of Spalding, still

His Royal Highness the Prince of Wales, as a young shepherd. A statue by Thomas and Mary Thorneycroft of Hampstead.

conducted its proceedings according to the 'Oeconomical Rule' adopted in 1710, which made very pleasant reading:

The Society must assemble at 4.

When the season requires there must be a Table, 2 candles, a pair of Snuffers, and a good Fire during the Society.

There must be a pot of Coffee of an ounce to eight dishes, or in proportion; there must be a pot of Bohea Tea of half an oz. to 12 dishes.

There must be 12 clean Pipes and an oz. of the best Tobacco.

There must be a Chamber Pot.

There must be a Latin Dictionary and a Greek Lexicon.

The Coffee and Tea must be ready exactly at five and taken away before six, which done the Papers must be read by some member.

Then a tankard of Ale holding one quart and no more must be set on the table.

The President must always sit on the right side of the chimney and take care of the Fire.

The members felt it their duty to travel down to the town of Boston, to see the 'Boston Stump', the tower which had for centuries been a landmark. The Lincoln to Boston railway line was not yet finished, and they might have had to travel by stage-coach, had not the Company been aware of the uses of advertisement. It cleaned up the 'earth waggons' which were being used to bring the foundations for the track, sat the archaeologists in them on benches, and ran a special train for them before the line was officially open.[173] It is likely enough that the members were more interested in this journey than the antiquity they had gone to inspect. The story of revolutions, the fates of kings and the speeches of Parliamentarians occupy, and must occupy, great space in history, but it is at least possible that more interest was felt at the time in facts such as that the railways had at last joined England and Scotland. London was now only thirteen hours from Glasgow or Edinburgh. On Brunel's special wide-gauge line the express called 'The Great Britain' took forty-seven minutes to cover the fifty-three miles between London and Didcot.[174] (Fastest time in 1954: sixty-eight minutes.) Felix Summerley's

Iron Road Books (6*d*. and 1*s*.), which were combinations of guide-books and time-tables, described journeys from London to Brighton, Tunbridge Wells, Wolverton, Gosport, Folkestone, Dover, Birmingham, Rugby and so forth, expanding the series as the railroads spread, and always listing not only the mansions and churches which the passenger should notice on his journey, but also the 'stations, viaducts, tunnels, gradients, etc.', which were at least as thrilling. No less than 1,800 miles of 'Electric Telegraph' (operated inefficiently, for the stationmasters were often afraid of it) ran alongside part of the 5,000 miles of railroad.[175] Navigators ('navvies' was a vulgar word) went in platoons about Britain building the railways. They wore white felt hats, velveteen square-tailed coats, scarlet plush waistcoats with little black spots, and corduroy breeches; they drank whisky by the tumbler and called it 'white beer'.[176] A chaplain questioned by the Parliamentary Commission on Railway Labourers about their morals gave an answer illuminating the opinions of his class as much as their habits:

Q. You speak of infidel opinions. Do you believe that many of them are Socialists?

A. Most of them, in practice. Though they appear to have wives, very few are married.[177]

VIII

September and October

*

THE most important political news in September, as
few Englishmen would have doubted, was the
death of a man whom no one except some race-
course swindlers disliked and for whom everyone had a
warm if rather indulgent respect. Even the man who
most benefited by it, Benjamin Disraeli, heard of the
death of Lord George Bentinck, the Conservative leader,
with genuine distress. Lord George appeared to be in
ruddy health and there was nothing unusual about his
behaviour on September 21st, the day of his death, except
that he refused any lunch. About four o'clock he
set out to walk to the house of a neighbouring peer, Lord
Manvers, where he was going to stay for two days; he
never arrived there. Late that night a search was made,
and he was found lying dead on his face near to a water-
meadow. He had bled at the nose from his fall, but there
was no other sign of violence and he had 'a cheerful
smile upon his face'. The cause of death was to some
extent mysterious; his heart was found to be 'completely
contracted' and contained no blood whatever. The
coroner's jury returned a rather antiquated and strange
verdict: 'Died by the visitation of God.' But whatever
its cause, and however widely it was regretted, Lord
George's death had for its chief result to force the Conservative Party to make a choice it had no inclination for
– the choice of a new leader. There was no candidate

who could even remotely compare with the flamboyant Jew whom the members of Parliament instinctively resented as much as they admired. Lord Stanley, the Tory leader in the Lords, whose eminence was chiefly due to birth and bad manners, made an attempt to avoid what he saw coming. Though he detested Disraeli and had done all he could to block his career, he forced his

SKETCH ON THE WELBECK ESTATE.

[Scene of the Death of Lord George Bentinck]

pen to write an effusive letter, and one which he thought was highly diplomatic. He was paying Disraeli, he wrote, 'the higher compliment', that of suggesting he should serve under 'a leader of inferior abilities', Mr. J. C. Herries, M.P. A foolish letter to send a man many times as skilled as he was in politics, it called for and immediately received a suave answer disclaiming any desire for leadership and announcing a realization that the writer would be more useful 'acting alone and un-shackled'. The letter brought the bull-headed peer abruptly up against the fact that Mr. Disraeli was essential; his last effort was to secure that the leadership was handed to a triumvirate of Mr. Disraeli, Mr. Herries and another nullity named Lord Granby. The day after the names were announced the effect of this was clear to all. 'It is the Consulate that came before the Empire,' said Aberdeen, the Whig leader. 'Look at the names – they are Napoleon Bonaparte, Roger Ducos and the Abbe Sieyès.' So they were; the second two vanished from the scene, and in a few weeks Disraeli was able to write to a friend the words which had for long been his ambition: 'I am fairly the leader.'[178] The largest and most obstinate conservative party in the civilized world had chosen as its chief a man who wrote like Oscar Wilde and looked like Ikey Moe; he was to lead it all his life and to impress on it principles which the members who originally accepted him not merely would not have liked, but would not even have understood.

The month that in this odd way saw the opening of a new political era also saw the closing of an old one. Disraeli imposed upon a selfish and unintelligent party of country landlords a mixture of romantic imperialism and social reform; it may or may not have been profoundly imprinted, but it saved the Tory Party from extinction and altered the history of Britain; it began a new epoch, if not for the country as a whole, at least for its governing class. The trials that opened the day after Lord George's death were the last words of the last chapter in an epoch of the history of the working class. The portrait of the sedate, sensible, solid British working man is not one that now can be painted out. But nobody would have recognized it as a true one in 1848. Until this year, the common man in England had been more turbulent, not less turbulent, than the common man elsewhere;

more revolutionary, not more stable. He had cut off the head of his King and established a republic 125 years earlier than anyone else had done such a thing, and when James II tried to recover the royal power had thrown him out with an insolent ease. The oppressions, the robberies and the cruelties which historians record of the eighteenth century and the Regency had as their other side the almost limitless personal liberty and freedom from interference that the poorer Englishman enjoyed in his cottage, garret or slum – a liberty which included the right to riot and misbehave violently. The landlords stole the commons and the mills ruined the weavers, but still, as his songs show, the free working man despised the Russian, Turk, Spaniard or Frenchman who trembled before a despot. The peaceful eviction of the old aristocracy from power by the Reform Bill of 1832 had only been possible because the Lords knew that certain men named Jones and Parkes and Place could call on 'the people', who would turn the country upside down in a week. Even after the Bill was passed, the town workers had shown their discontent by a monstrous attempt to organize what was called a 'general turn-out' – a proposal merely to walk away from society and so cause the whole of organized life to crash. It was fortunately unsuccessful, but it was a thing which had never been attempted before, if one discounted a probably legendary story about ancient Rome 2,329 years before. No one suspected that this people was about to become the most law-abiding in the world, and that in thirteen years' time one of their most incessant sermonizers, Richard Cobden, would find himself appalled at what he called their 'meekness'. But it was so; so complete was the break with the revolutionary past that

the trial which now opened, and which once would have
been as long remembered and resented as that of Sacco
and Vanzetti, was totally forgotten. The Social-
Democrats in the 1880s and the Communists in the
1920s, passionately searching history for propaganda,
never even found it.

When Dr. McDouall, on the past Whit-Monday,
decided to adjourn the Chartist insurrection for two
months, he had made two mistakes. He had thought
that a revolutionary army could be retained intact like
a regular army, and that the police would continue to be
inactive. But during these two months of depressing
news the Chartist ranks began to dwindle, and he had to
look for other recruits. The only helpers he could find
were what were called the Confederates, which was the
name taken by the Irish revolutionaries over in England.
They were poor material; they did too little and they
talked too much. Particularly the latter: they could
never hold their tongues, and some at least of them were
in with the police as well. Their chief at first was a man
called Macmanus, sent over 'by the Irish Republic',
but promptly caught by a detective at a Chartist meeting
in Dean Street Assembly Rooms; he escaped by throwing
the detective downstairs, but had to hand over to a
painter named Dowling, who was almost as great a
chatterbox.[179]   The Chartist chiefs themselves were
nearly as imprudent; Ernest Jones, the lawyer who
was gradually taking O'Connor's place, had publicly
outlined the military organization that was being per-
fected – by 'classes' of nine under a 'class leader', nine
class-leaders being under a 'ward-mate' – and thereafter as near as might be indicated the time when it
would be called on to act.[180]   It was not really surprising

that the police put him, McDouall, and the expert fighter, Fussell, in jail, leaving only the lesser leaders at large. They also took another precaution, which came out at the trial.

The day chosen for revolt was August 16th; the last

A PHYSICAL FORCE CHARTIST. ARMING FOR THE FIGHT.

briefing meeting was held on Monday the 14th, at which each ward-mate was required to report on the numbers whom he could answer for on the day. The figures had fallen away depressingly; faced with an exact demand, the ward-mates could only be sure of between 500 and 600 armed and drilled men. The total of London Chartists of all kinds, who might or might not join in, had fallen to 5,000 – half what it had once been. There were probably as many more 'Confederates', but their value was doubtful. All the same, it was decided to go forward; for it was surely a case of 'now or never'. The Committee consisted of Cuffay, the mulatto tailor, Rose, who had been in the Whit-Monday affair, Ritchie, a plasterer, Mullins, a young surgeon of twenty-two, a man called Fay, Lacey, a shoemaker, and Johnson, a professional walker known as 'The Welsh Novice'. Ritchie had a special corps of 'luminaries' who were experts in arson, but the driving force was largely Johnson. 'I am sick of all your talking', he cried. He had cast bullets and rolled cartridges; he had even designed and made 'caltrops', iron balls with four spikes which would be thrown down to make cavalry charges impossible, as they had done at Bannockburn.[181] There seems to have been some latent hesitation still; Mullins, in the chair, would not announce outright that Ritchie's men should fire the mains, but said: 'If I look at the gas, you will all know what I mean.'[182] The Committee was to sit all day Wednesday at the Orange Tree Inn, near to Red Lion Square, to direct the revolt. The revolutionary troops would fall in at four places: Clerkenwell Green (Brewster commanding), Tower Hamlets (Payne), Broadway in Westminster (Dr. Mullins) and Seven Dials, also in Westminster (Bassett).[183]

The Committee had duly assembled on the day, Johnson being absent. Before any reports could be received from the four commanders, a detachment of police had marched up to the Orange Tree Inn and arrested everybody. For Johnson had been a police agent all the time, and now he faced them in court under his real name of Powell. He had worked up the insurrection for pay; it was as simple as that. Under cross-examination, he made a poor showing: 'utterly depraved' was a friendly verdict. Counsel for the defence, an unbalanced man named Edward Kenealy, did all that fury could suggest, even threatening to assault the Attorney-General, but there could be no doubt of the result. The sentences were to long terms of deportation, except, of course, for Johnson, who was given a good sum of money to go to Australia. (He returned next year, asking for more.)[184]

What happened to the four waiting Chartist regiments when their headquarters was captured? It so happens that in one case we know; there was an eyewitness. It was the last attempt ever made at a revolution in Britain, and though perhaps unimportant in itself, it has at least a curiosity value, like a rare stamp. Here is the report; it concerns Seven Dials, which is a run-down place where seven streets join, and where in 1848 there was a pub on every corner.

While these arrests were being made, about one hundred and fifty men were assembled on the Seven Dials – standing in groups at the street corners or before the bars of the public houses. Just after the arrests at the Orange Tree a man approached a group at the corner of Great St. Andrew Street and spoke a few hurried words in a low voice to a labourer who, with a pickaxe in his hand, was directing the attention of his companions to a loose stone in the pavement of the roadway. Almost at the same moment a body of police made their appearance, but apparently without any other intention than being in readiness for something. The man moved quickly from one group to another and as he left each the men composing it separated, some walking quietly away and others entering the public houses at the corners of the streets to communicate what they had heard to those assembled inside. In this manner the number of men assembled on the Dials was reduced in a few minutes to about a tenth of those who had been found there.[185]

That was all. That was the end of the story; there never would be anything more to add to it.

Little notice was taken of it; little, also, was taken of an event at the other end of Europe, which it would have been wise to have watched. What was later named Rumania was at this time divided into two principalities called Moldavia and Wallachia, nominally under the rule of the Sultan of Turkey, but also under the protection of the Tsar of Russia. The Moldavians and the Wallacks had demanded and secured the usual constitution, with free speech, a parliament, freedom of the person and even land reform. Now Russian troops, with the consent of Turkey, were sent in, seeped over the land in a great grey flood, and stamped out all liberty, putting the two princes back on their thrones. It was the first time that heavy, barbarous mass had advanced. The Tsar also took another action which it was less easy to ignore. He informed the King of Prussia that he disapproved of the Prussian action over Schleswig-Holstein. It was condoning a rebellion by subjects against a King, and this could not be allowed in any circumstances. The implied menace coincided with the King's own misgivings. The Prussian army had defeated the Danish

army and occupied Jutland, but the Danish navy had
control of the Baltic and was blockading the Prussian
ports. It was expensive and most inconvenient, and for
whose advantage, Frederick William asked himself, was
he putting up with this inconvenience? For a free,
united and democratic Germany, replied in effect the
Frankfort Parliament, which had adopted the war as its
own child and as 'an affair of German honour'. No
answer could be less pleasing and less convincing to the
King; saying nothing to the German Parliament, he
came to an arrangement with the King of Denmark by
which he quitted the war and the Danish King continued as Duke of Schleswig and Holstein. There was a
burst of fury in the Frankfort Parliament; after a wild
debate it voted not to accept the armistice. By that vote
it showed to itself and its enemies the second great
weakness of the revolutionary movement. Neither it,
nor any of the German and Austrian Parliaments, had
secured control of the armed forces. It had no troops
with which to back its angry words. Nor could it now
raise any. Perhaps, in the days of March, the Prussian,
Hessian, Bavarian, Austrian and other assemblies might
have secured control of the local armies; perhaps not.
It was an unquestioned tradition in every country
except Britain that the army's loyalty was a personal
loyalty to the sovereign; if there had been any doubts
behind the uniforms earlier, there were none now. In a
few days' time Parliament realized this, swallowed
'German honour' and unhappily reversed its vote. Then
the spectators in the galleries decided to play their part.
The people of Paris, listening to the debates, had forced
the Convention in 1793 to take revolutionary decisions,
and had expelled the traitors; they would do the same.

Led by clubs like the Paris clubs, the people of Frankfort, or some of them at least, attacked Parliament House intending to purge it. They failed; Parliament was rescued after a sharp struggle (by Prussian troops). All that they did was to kill pretty brutally Prince Lichnowsky, the playboy of the extreme Right – and even this murder was a stupid one, for the Prince had learned sense and tolerance almost against his will while he was in the House, and was rapidly changing into a constitutionalist. Finally, since all tragedies must have a clown, Hecker's vegetarian lieutenant, Struve, chose this moment to stage a fresh invasion of Germany through Baden, and to be bundled out again equally ignominiously.

If there was no strength left in Frankfort, was there any in the other two German capitals, Vienna and Berlin? Not in Berlin; King Frederick William now knew his strength and, since nothing bound him but his own promises, decided to restore his own autocracy. The process took a few weeks; he first substituted a Conservative Cabinet for a Liberal one, then ordered the Parliament to meet in Brandenburg instead of Berlin, finally sent Count von Wrangel, who had been his general in Schleswig-Holstein, to shut down Parliament altogether. The Parliamentary leader was a man named von Unruh, and under his direction the members opposed passive resistance to what, in their simple-minded way, they called violence and treachery. 'Go on – break the laws and steal,' said one of them named Jacoby to Major the Count von Blumenthal, as his soldiers forced them out of the hall and grabbed the Parliamentary journals. 'Some day you will be made to answer for this.'

'Gentlemen, do not embarrass me,' said the Count, an uneasiness passing through his mind. He need not have worried; the Prussian Parliamentarians were indeed as courageous as Pym or Hampden, on whom they were modelling themselves, but the nation to whom they appealed was not listening.[186]

Unexpectedly enough, the Austrians and Hungarians

MAGYAR DEPUTY.   MAGNATE IN FULL NATIONAL DRESS.   HUNGARIAN HUSSAR.   GRENADIER AND FUSILIER OFFICERS.   ROYAL HUNGARIAN INFANTRY.

were tougher than the Prussians. The Austrian Emperor, Ferdinand, or perhaps his advisers, decided that the time had now come when the reformers could be put down. He thought, probably rightly, that the Hungarians were the most dangerous of those whom he considered all to be rebels; he therefore on October 3rd dissolved the Hungarian Assembly and appointed Count Jellachich to be ruler of Hungary. This was an outrage to the romantic Hungarians in that it was a complete repudiation of his promises to his loyal people and a breach of rights and privileges which they had had for some 500 years, but it was a far greater outrage because of the man who was chosen. Count Jellachich was the leader – the 'Ban', as he was called – of Croatia, and had been for some time engaged in intermittent warfare against the Hungarians. If the Hungarians had been wiser, there need have been no Croat revolts, no doubt; but they were still living partly in a medieval world, where they believed the Emperor lived too. Croatia was a part of Hungary and the Ban was a rebel; the Emperor had granted Hungary a constitution; they had been loyally grateful and obedient to him; he had more than once officially rebuked the Ban Jellachich for not being the same towards them. The Hungarian Parliament could hardly believe the news; Count Batthanyi, its leader, resigned in shame and handed over power to Louis Kossuth, who had been regarded as too extreme.

The perfidy – the word was commonly used in Budapest and it is exact enough – the perfidy of the Emperor Ferdinand had one good effect in that it ended indecision in the minds of a great many Hungarians whose thoughts were occupied with questions of homage, loyalty, truth and duty which would have seemed anti-quated further west. Loyalty could no longer be owed to an Emperor who broke his word and nominated as ruler a man whom he had recently called a traitor. They were therefore prepared to move against him, and once they were so prepared, they moved as one block, without divisions within the nation. The Home Guard – Honveds, a name which became famous, means only Home Guards – drove Jellachich's armies out of town after town; each farmer, peasant, or farm labourer had his horse, sword and rifle, and on these wide plains were a swiftly manœuvring force for which the Ban was quite unprepared. Kossuth made two military appointments, one excellent and one disastrous. He chose as chief commander Arthur Görgei, a bluff, sergeant-major type of officer who appeared to be devoted to Hungarian democracy; as a lesser commander, with duties in the east and particularly in Transylvania, he selected Bem, one of the many Polish generals who were wandering about Europe hoping to be employed in the cause of freedom. No more brilliant commander could have been chosen. Bem reconquered the whole of that great province in a matter of weeks. He outmanœuvred and defeated the forces opposed to him (among which he saw with disquiet some Russian regiments that had no business there), and he destroyed the bases on which they relied by enforcing justice for Wallacks and Slavs. While he was in command, all persecution of these subordinate races was prevented, and they were allowed their share of the freedoms which had been secured. He was equally intelligent and humane in dealing with his own troops; he could on occasion be merciless, as when he told an officer who said a position could not be held, 'You will hold it, or you will be shot,' but more typical is his speech to a Honved levy which had broken and fled. He told them that he could have had them shot or flogged; he would not shoot them, because he believed that they might still serve their country; he would not flog them, because he would not treat them as beasts; therefore he had no choice but to forgive them. They were ever afterwards a crack unit in his army.[187] Görgei, on the other hand, was slow, suspicious, and sullen; his efficiency was confined to details, and his democratic principles were non-existent – he was merely discontented and ambitious. When, and if, disaster came, these faults could be fatal.

For the moment, however, the Hungarian revolution was healthy and strong, an untroubled extrovert among neurotics. Elsewhere, there was disaster. The Viennese attempted to defy the Emperor, who fled from the city and instructed Prince Windischgrätz to reduce it to obedience. Windischgrätz, the man who believed that

BOHEMIAN OFFICER OF THE ARTILLERY.   OFFICER OF INFANTRY.   GENERAL IN FULL DRESS, BEARING THE ORDER OF MARIA-THERESA.   CUIRASSIER OF THE IMPERIAL GUARD.   REGULAR CROATIAN INFANTRY.

human beings began at barons, was glad of the assignment, and attacked the capital vigorously. The Viennese fought well, and the Hungarians came to their aid – but ineffectively. Their general, Moga (Kossuth's appointments had not yet come into effect), was troubled about crossing the frontier without an official permit, and by the time he had advanced twice and retired twice Windischgrätz was well enough entrenched to defeat him. The fall of Vienna followed almost at once; Windischgrätz's firing squads, in making an end of the students and workers who had caused the trouble originally, also seized and killed one of the ablest and most disinterested of the members of the Frankfort Parliament whom they found there, Robert Blum by name. There was an outcry among those who still believed in parliaments, freedom and humanity; but it was a vain outcry. The murder of Robert Blum, they said, was symbolical; it was so, intentionally.

Austrian rule was being restored in Northern Italy by the same means. Marshal Radetzky was shooting selectively but quite mercilessly in the towns which he had re-taken after the flight of Charles Albert, which included all the big cities except Venice. The killings in Milan were especially callous, and Lord Palmerston instructed the British Ambassador in Vienna to represent to the Austrian Court that they were a 'flagrant and palpable violation of the truce' which the Marshal had signed in order to get an easy entry to the city. Prince Schwarzenberg, for the Emperor, sent back an insulting answer, of which Palmerston said it was 'the outpourings of a woman of the streets arrested by a policeman in the act of picking a pocket'.[188] The phrase may have consoled him, but it was inexact. The policeman had not arrested the harlot, who still was picking pockets. Great Britain could not or would not do anything; her angriest Note was less important than a private word from Russia.

Some of the reasons for the defeats of the forces of freedom in the later months of 1848 have been already suggested – the appearance of the 'proletarian revolt', the failure to take control of the armies early on, the quarrels between nationalities, but one of the most effective is not mentioned in political history. It was cholera. There is no disease, today, which has the terrifying character of cholera. It was as death-dealing and unexplained as cancer; it came with the relentless periodicity of polio. It produced the same helpless despair as would an epidemic of those two diseases combined, with the additional effect that even those who did not die were left inert and exhausted. As town after town was struck down by it, the inhabitants were in no mood to resist tyranny by gallantly running up great barricades; a sort of Oriental apathy was more likely to overcome them, and the silence with which the appeals of the Parliaments was received was in part really the silence of the dead.

The disease's first appearance was sometimes deceptively mild; the symptom was a slight and painless diarrhœa, which the victim treated (if he followed the advice of the Board of Health in London) with opium, brandy and water, or a chalk mixture. Soon, however, the diarrhœa became profuse and watery, and the patient vomited great quantities of watery fluid. His appearance was unmistakable and frightful. Dark circles ringed his eyes, his skin was cold and clammy, he writhed in muscular cramps, he lay moaning in a helpless prostration, his pulse had almost disappeared. He appeared shrunken; indeed, he was shrunken – his body was drying up, he would evacuate as much as 'eight pints or more' of liquid in two or three hours, and vomit as much as a quart at a time.[189] Often he died of a 'dry collapse', his body desiccated, while his bowels were found full of fluid. Treatment was ineffective; the three commonest remedies were opiates, bleeding and purging, and of all three there were many doctors who said they were more disastrous than helpful. The 'comma' bacillus was not to be discovered until 1883; meanwhile, the most various theories of the disease's origin were seriously discussed, and contradictory régimes prescribed in consequence. Dr. Charles Cowdell considered it was spread by fungi; Dr. Leared that it arose from electricity, noting that the telegraph was deranged in St. Petersburg during the epidemic and that the body of a dying girl gave off sparks; Dr. Billing held that it was nothing but an ordinary fever. While some doctors bled their patients, the Senior Physician at St. George's Hospital injected blood as a remedy. Others held that it was caused by a lesion of the brain affecting the nerves communicating with the bowels, or that it was spread by 'animalculae' or 'miasmas', Dr. Farr showing in support of the last view that it was most common in low-lying and wet areas.[190] The Press, on the authority of the *Lancet*, urged the removal of rubbish, the clearing of drains, the exposure of bedding to the sun, 'dry scrubbing' of the home without the use of water, the breaking down of partitions to improve ventilation, and the wearing of a red flannel belt round the belly.[191] The official instructions issued in October in general confirmed this advice. Cholera, they said, throve in damp and low-lying districts; any dampness must therefore be attacked and any decomposing material be removed, because it led to 'atmospheric impurity'.[192] For, the Board added, affecting a confidence it did not really have, cholera was proved not to be contagious, but was spread by the air. Army orders in India required (and for years continued to require) that regiments should march 'at right angles to the wind', to outwit the disease.[193]

The cholera epidemic of 1848 had advanced with a slow and lumbering certainty which terrified those who were watching. It came from Asia, and its progress is recorded.[194] It broke out in Chinese Turkestan and in Bokhara in 1844. In 1845 it spread steadily southwards into Persia, Afghanistan and India. In 1846 it turned west, reaching Bagdad and going slowly up the Tigris to Diarbekr. In 1847 it reached Russia, arriving in Moscow via Tiflis, the Crimea and Saratoff. In July, 1848 there were between 400 and 500 deaths daily in St. Petersburg, out of a population of around half a million.[195] Watching the plague slowly moving westward across Europe, both British and American doctors hoped that the seas would stop it, but knew really that they would not. 'Cholera is expected soon' said the chief Washington paper resignedly, and gave one-fifth of its space to advice on how to deal with it, no more useful than the British prescriptions.[196] The New York Homoeopathic Board of Trustees, and other bodies, arranged for repeated public lectures, which were reprinted in full by the anxious press.[197] By September, Hamburg was being desolated by cholera and, as had been feared, it was soon brought across the North Sea by unknown means to London. Next month it came to Edinburgh, and here the transmitters were known – three sailors who died of it soon after landing. The Board of Health, anxiously seeking for a light on the cause of the disease, called on the public to observe that before leaving Hamburg the three men had 'exceeded' on plums and sour beer.[198] For whatever reason, the epidemic thus started in the north was more virulent than the attack in London: 119 places were attacked; 53,293 people died; the deaths in Hull were one in 1,000 of the population. From Edinburgh the disease spread to Belfast, and, with little more than a month's delay, to

what the British papers still spelled 'Staaten Island';
by December 17th it had broken out in New Orleans
and was going up the Mississippi. It turned along the
Ohio River and reached as far as Cincinnati.[199]

During this dismal period there was what appeared to
be one item of cheerful news. In the second week of
October the papers printed a letter which had been
despatched to the Admiralty in April by Chief Factor
Macpherson in the Hudson's Bay Company's territory
in Canada, and had only just arrived. It said that the
Peel River Eskimos had seen two large boats to the east
of the Mackenzie River, full of white men. If this were
true 'there is reason to believe the expedition is out of
danger'.[200] This was the last news ever received of
Sir John Franklin's expedition to find the North-West
Passage, and it was false.

The anxiety with which information was awaited
arose partly from the object of the expedition, but even
more from the character of its chief, who was held in
affection and respect by almost all who knew him or
knew of him. The statue of him in Waterloo Place today
gives him a false appearance of majesty. He was short,
fat, gentle, cheerful, rather deaf, energetic, and almost
bouncy. His portrait by Negelin shows his character
far better, with his bald head cocked back slightly like a
bird's and a confident smile on its broad face. The
decorations with which his post-captain's uniform is
studded were well earned. He had fought under Nelson
at Copenhagen and at Trafalgar. Apart from his war
service, he had commanded or taken part in naval
exploration expeditions which had been unequalled
in their success – he had explored Spitzbergen to the
east and to the west had discovered no less than 1,200

miles of sea-coast between the Bering Straits and the
Mackenzie River, on the Arctic coast of Canada. On
land he had spent three years in the wild northern
wastes of the same country, and seen his savage and half-
savage companions turn in their misery to cannibalism
and murder.[201] For the value of his reports he had been
made a Fellow of the Royal Society, for his devotion
and courage he had been given various official duties,
the latest being the Governorship of Tasmania, still called
Van Diemen's Land. Here he became entangled in
the intrigues of a new and petty colonial society; there
were two opinions of his services, and Lord Stanley, the
then Colonial Secretary, with his usual rudeness, sent a
successor out as Governor without notifying him, and on
his return refused him either explanation or rehabilita-
tion. Official[202] circles felt guilty over this crass behaviour, and the next year – 1845 – had been unable to
resist his pleas to be given an authorization and an
expedition to fulfil his dearest hope – to find a North-
West Passage. 'But, you know, Sir John,' said the First
Lord of the Admiralty, Lord Haddington, doubtfully,
'we know your age – you are sixty.'

'No, no, my lord!' said the plump little man, jumping
from his chair. 'Not quite, my lord!' (He must have
been fifty-nine and some months.)

'Are you sure your constitution will bear it?' continued Lord Haddington.

'You will examine me! You will examine me!' said
Sir John, repeating it again and again.[203]

A glance at a map of the Canadian Arctic as it was
when Franklin set out is needed to show what was meant
by the search for the North-West Passage. Essentially
the aim was, of course, to find a sea-way round the

north of the American continent, as Magellan had found a way round the south 400 years before. Recent explorations, many of them Franklin's own, had pushed great tongues of discovery into the unknown regions. But they had never met; there was still a resistant belt of unexplored darkness, so narrow as to be tantalizing. If only his expedition could get as far west as longitude 125

The Search for the North-West Passage. Extent of Explored Areas about the year 1848.

and spend the winter there, then Franklin was almost certain he could discover a passage, although, of course, there was a chance that the whole dark block might turn out to be solid land and part of the continent.

The Admiralty gave him what he asked for – two excellently constructed ships, the *Erebus* and the *Terror*, each with 50-horse-power engines and admirable crews; and he set off to the north, sailing towards the gulf between Baffin Land and Greenland. He had not been heard from again, and though the passing of one winter

without news was of no importance, the silence through
the winter of 1847-8 was disquieting. Lady Franklin,
who for many years refused to believe in her husband's
death, had badgered the admiralty into sending an
expedition of rescue headed by Sir James Ross. So far
the messages coming back had only been: 'No news yet
of Sir John Franklin.'[204] Ross carried the first of many
letters from Lady Franklin to her husband:

> MY DEAREST LOVE, May it be the will of God, if you
> are not restored to us earlier, that you should open
> this letter and that it may give you comfort in all
> your trials. . . .

Nobody but herself was in fact to open it; like its many
successors, it came back unread, bearing the news that
once would have entertained him:

> Louis Philippe is dethroned and an exile in England,
> a fierce democracy ruling France, almost all the
> Kingdoms of Europe in commotion, England alone
> steady and erect.

There were the trivialities which seem so pathetic
when they are re-read months later and their uselessness
known – in this case, plans for a little property at
Clavering

> which will furnish us with two or three rooms to
> which to retire when we wish to ruralize. If there
> is to be any more book-writing, it will be good for a
> retreat and at all events I think you will be glad of a
> little place to which to run occasionally. . . . I will
> leave any forgotten or unmentioned things for Sir
> James to tell you – I have written in a great
> hurry.[205]

Sir James Ross was searching in the wrong parts of the Arctic; 'it was 1859 before the right place was searched, and little was to be found there but metal objects, and wisps of clothing, and human bones'.[206] It did not matter; it was already too late.

Franklin and his expedition had spent their first winter on the little island called Beechey Isle, beyond the farthest point of Baffin Land. The winter seems to have been busy and happy, with but one disaster; over 700 tins of meat provided by a contractor named Goldner were found to be putrid.[207] After making a circle to the north and proving that the land to his west was part of an island, called Cornwallis Island, Franklin correctly decided that they should turn south and hope to strike a way through to that part of the sea which was known to exist at the mouth of Back's Fish River. What happened thereafter was first made known when a paper was discovered long afterwards in a cairn upon the island called King William's Land, by which the North-West Passage passes today. The paper is blue, is 12½ inches long by 8 inches, stained, and with one corner torn off. It is a printed form issued by the Admiralty asking 'whoever finds this paper' to return it to the Admiralty saying when and where it was found, and repeating this request in French, Spanish, Dutch, Danish and German. On the upper part of the form is written in a firm flowing hand:

H.M. Ships *Erebus* and *Terror*.
28 of May 1847. Wintered in the ice in Lat. 70° 5′ N., Long. 90° 23′ W.
  Having wintered in 1846-7 at Beechey Island in Lat 74° 43′ 28″ N., Long. 91° 39′ 13″ W. After

having ascended Wellington Channel to Lat. 77° and returned by the west side of Cornwallis Island. Sir John Franklin commanding the expedition. All well.

At the bottom are the words: 'Party consisting of 2 officers and 6 men left the ships on Monday 24th May, 1847. Gm. Gore, Lieut. Ch. F. Des Voeux, Mate.' The first signatory was 'sweet-tempered Graham Gore', Franklin's second-in-command.[208] He had made a mistake in writing '1846-47' for '1845-46' in his report which was to confuse historians for years to come.

Round the sides and top, in a straggling and weak handwriting, is a later message, written when the paper had been taken out of its resting place and replaced:

April 25 1848. H.M. Ships *Erebus* and *Terror* were deserted on April 22, five leagues N.N.W. of this, having been beset since September 1846. The officers and crew, consisting of 105 souls, under the command of Captain F. R. M. Crozier, landed here in latitude 63° 37' 42" N., longitude 98° 41' W. . . . Sir John Franklin died on June 11 1847, and the total loss by death in the expedition has been, up to this date, nine officers and fifteen men. Start on tomorrow, 26th, for Back's Fish River.

They set off, and were never seen alive again. There were grim charts made later, of places now bearing such names as 'Crozier Cape' and 'Graham Inlet', on which were marked *Skeleton here* showing how far some of the men reached, and a boat was found with two bodies in it, one still holding a rifle and the other with a New Testament in what had been a pocket, with the initials

'G. G.' on it. They had not failed, for they had discovered the North-West Passage – they must have seen
it from the turn of King William's Land and may even,
as the biographers hoped, have told Sir John of this
before he died.[209] Perhaps, indeed, it is wrong to say
they were never seen again; an old Eskimo woman
spoke of seeing some white men 'very thin and seeming
in want of provisions' in this summer of 1848, who 'fell
down and died as they walked along'. She may really
have seen them; there is a vividness about the phrase
which seems authentic, or she may have made up the
story to please the inquirers.[210]

There was news, this month of October, from another
naval officer of the same rank as Sir John – post-captain
– but of an amusing and not of a grim character. It was
probably inevitable that a year of wonders like 1848
could not pass by without an account of a sea-serpent
more serious than the tall story from Vermont. The
writer was Peter M'Quhae, commander of H.M.S.
Daedalus, and his report to the Admiralty (made at their
request) was dated October 11th:

At 5 o'clock p.m. on the 6th August last, in lat.
24° 44′ S. and long. 9° 22′ E. [that is, in the South
Atlantic] something very unusual was seen by Mr.
Sartoris, midshipman, rapidly approaching the ship
from before the beam. It was discovered to be an
enormous serpent, with head and shoulders kept
about 4 feet constantly above the surface of the sea;
and as nearly as we could approximate by compar-
ing it with the length of our maintopsail yard . . .
there was at the very least 60 ft. of the animal *à
fleur d'eau* [at water-level].

The midshipman reported it to the officer of the watch, Lieut. Edgar Drummond 'with whom and with Mr. William Barrett, the Master, I was at the time walking the quarter-deck'. It passed rapidly and did not appear to be 'propelled by either vertical or horizontal undulation'. It was so close that 'had it been a man of my acquaintance I should easily have recognized his

THE SEA-SERPENT WHEN FIRST SEEN FROM H.M.S. "DÆDALUS."

features'. Its face was undoubtedly a snake's, however. It paid no attention to the ship and went on its very determined way at about twelve or fifteen miles an hour; it was dark-brown with a yellowish-white throat; it had no fins and had a sort of mane washing about its back. The quartermaster, the bos'n's mate, and the man at the wheel saw it as well as the officers; the ship's company as a whole did not, being at supper. A drawing was made of it immediately, and this was published in the *Illustrated London News*.[211] The monster had been seen from other ships about the same time, but not so closely, nor had it been described by witnesses of such un-questioned honesty and competence.

The report was greeted with scepticism, as such reports are, and Professor Richard Owen, F.R.S., inter-vened to explain it away. It was, he said, a very large seal which had floated down on an iceberg; the iceberg

THE GREAT POLITICAL SEA SERPENT

had melted underneath it and it was, in a naturally preoccupied manner, paddling away furiously to get back to something solid. What the various officers and men had imagined to be a continuation of the animal was in fact only the eddy produced by the animal because it was so very large and was proceeding so very fast. Professor Owen's reputation since those days has suffered a decline, for he was the chief opponent of Darwin's theory of evolution and combated it by statements which now appear to be bigoted where they are not silly;[212]

but at this time he was at the height of his fame, and he seems to have disposed of the story. Captain M'Quhae, much of whose life had been spent among seals, was extremely annoyed at the suggestion that he would have failed to recognize one, and other officers, including Lieutenant Drummond, gave evidence to the effect that

RECREATIONS IN NATURAL HISTORY.

First Naturalist. "WHAT! THE S-S-SHE-SHER-PENT A-AN (HIC) ICH (HIC) THYO-SAURUS! NONSHE-ENSE!"
Second Naturalist. "WHO SAID ICH-(HIC) ICHTHY-O-SAURUS! I SAID A (HIC) PLESI-O-(HIC) SAURUS PLAINENUFF."

whatever might be the explanation, Professor Owen's theory was untenable.[213] Indeed, if it had been allowed that the existence of a sea-serpent at all was admissible, the evidence given would have proved it in any ordinary court of law; but it was not thought possible, and has not been since. The sea-serpent is, and must be, a fable. However, since in 1954 there was discovered the coelacanth, a sea-beast which was held to have been extinct

for a million years, it may be permissible to linger for a
moment over a letter in *The Times*, whose writer said
that what Captain M'Quhae had seen was a plesiosaurus.
This prehistoric monster, he stated, swam with only its
neck above water and moved by means of paddles or
fins, just as the Captain's sea-serpent did, and it almost
certainly had a similar mane, just as its descendant the
iguana has, which Professor Owen could have seen at the
Zoo.

IX

November

*

THERE were graver subjects in November for
Western attention than sea-serpents, but none that
brought back the acute anxiety of earlier months.
News from India showed that General Gough's scepticism had been better founded than Governor-General
Dalhousie's optimism. As soon as it was seen that the
fortress of Multan would not fall forthwith, the allegedly
loyal Sikh forces under Shere Singh had promptly
changed sides, joined the Mulraj and attacked the
British. A full-scale new Sikh war had started; Lord
Dalhousie characteristically greeted it with a boastful
proclamation, saying, 'I have drawn the sword and
thrown away the scabbard!' General Gough had the less
theatrical task of breaking down the resistance of both
Sikh armies and forcing his way into Multan.[214] There
was to be no decisive battle within the year, but the
British forces reached the walls of Multan and almost
their first shots produced a sensational story for the
London papers.

Yesterday [wrote an eyewitness] I saw one of the
most awful and grand sights I am ever likely to
witness; the whole of the Mulraj's principal
magazine, which he has been five years collecting,
was blown up by one of our shells. The shock two
miles off knocked bottles off the table, and the

report was terrific. All his principal houses, temples, etc. as well as about 800 men were blown up. . . . At first we felt a slight shock, like that of an earthquake, and then a second or two afterwards such a tremendous and prolonged report that it was like an awful clap of thunder – I hardly know what to liken it to, it was so inconceivably grand. Then a mass of dust rose to the very clouds. So perfectly distinct was its outline, and it was so dense and thick, that it looked like an immense solid brown tree suddenly grown up to the skies; and then it gradually expanded and slowly sailed away.

The Mulraj, however, was not overwhelmed; when the British general followed this up with a demand for surrender, he pushed the letter down the muzzle of 'his longest gun' and fired it back at him.

If he was contumacious, it mattered very little; the Punjab was far away and the British public was confident that this little war would end as all little wars did, in the ultimate victory of the red-coats. Everything seemed to encourage the Victorians to fall back into their original contentment. There were still Chartist trials, reminding them of the existence of the discontented, but the revelations were less and less sensational and the sentences grew smaller and smaller. The bottom seemed to have been reached with the trial of Joseph Barker and others.[215] The Attorney-General moved that they all be discharged on condition of entering 'into their own recognizances' to appear if called upon. All of them were glad enough to be sent away so, except Barker, who was a man of principle. He insisted on being tried for high treason, he said; he had collected fifty witnesses to prove that this was a tyrannous prosecution and he would not see all his money and time wasted. 'This is morbid vanity,' said the judge, but he only provoked Barker to start delivering the speech from the dock which he had already prepared. After this grotesque scene had gone on half a day the judge and the Attorney-General gave way, and a verdict of acquittal was entered for Barker, without his fifty witnesses being called.

But if the restoration of order was a pleasant and soothing process to the English middle class, it was depressing and sometimes convulsive abroad. In Prussia the Parliament had been driven out, and the members were still practising passive resistance. In Frankfort the Assembly was powerless and some of the Assemblymen had, already, begun to slip off home. North Italy was reconquered and silent, except for Venice; so too was Vienna itself. All the same, the Emperor Ferdinand was persuaded by his Court to give way to somebody more firm-minded, who would make sure that no such insubordination ever occurred again in the Austro-Hungarian Empire. There was naturally some hesitation and argument, and the necessary decrees were not actually published until two days after the end of the month. But it was decided in November that he would abdicate in favour not of a direct successor but of his nephew, Francis Joseph, a boy of eighteen who was serving under Marshal Radetzky. These two, the very old man and the very young man, took into their hands the destiny of Austria-Hungary. Radetzky commanded the army for eleven more years, when he died at the age of ninety-two; Francis Joseph was Emperor until he died in 1916, in the middle of the first world war. At the time, they seemed to have been successful as no other partnership had ever been. They restored the 'Vienna régime' as it used to be; they put down every rebel; they outwitted every advocate of change. It is doubtful if either of them ever suspected that their rigidity had made the destruction of Austria-Hungary certain. Their first success was against Hungary; their reorganized armies secured several victories in the field.

(The victories were ephemeral. The story of the Hungarian revolution belongs to the year 1849; it can only be summarized here. As soon as Kossuth had organized them, the Hungarians chased the Imperial troops from town to town with the skilful rhythm of a Strauss waltz; they had wholly liberated their country when the Emperor called in the Russians. The Tsar sent in wave after wave of obedient grey-clothed serfs who drowned the Hungarian revolution in their unending mass until Görgei surrendered; for it was the fate of this picturesque nation to have its liberties twice strangled by Russian troops.)

It was difficult to classify the other most sensational event of the month. Was it a last victory for the spirit of reform – the traditional final flare before the candle guttered out? Or was it a mistimed blow for reaction? In the opinion of many circles in Britain and America – perhaps in a majority of the serious-minded – it was neither; it was the final proof that this year was the commencement of Armageddon. The year had begun – had it not? – with the destruction of nearly all the kingdoms of this earth, as was prophesied, and now, on November 24th, the Pope of Rome fled from the city upon seven hills. Whether he fled because he had to or because he thought it more skilful to do so, pious thinkers did not care; Protestant pulpits echoed to rejoicings at the fall of Antichrist and to careful, crazy calculations based on the Book of Revelation. The clergymen, however, were the only people who were certain; no one else knew what the Pope was doing, what he wanted, or where he was going. He had in the past few months accepted democratic ministries, but not sincerely, as it now appeared; recently he had replaced them by one headed by Pellegrino Rossi, a politician of thoroughly undemocratic principles, but a man of much better character than those around him. Rossi tried to reform the State finances, at the expense of the armies of clergy who lived off it, and even began to clear up the immense corruption of the Civil Service; he had deserved a better fate than he met, which was to be assassinated on November 15th.[216] Ten days later, without giving any indication to his next set of Ministers, the Pope stole away from the city. He had secured the help of the French Minister, who thought he was going to France, and announced this. But it was not so; he went to the fortress of Gaeta in the territory of Naples, for the protector he had chosen was King Ferdinand. Ferdinand had just secured the nickname of King Bomba, having brought his ships up to the defenceless port of Messina and bombarded it to ruins as part of his invasion of Sicily. What the Pope's intentions were is still not certain; he sent out messages requiring absolute submission from the Romans, and may well have considered that the shock of his disappearance would secure it. The calculation, in that case, was very nearly successful; there was a period of paralysis, and some at least of the poorer working class were terrified at his absence. But, as the days passed, it was seen to be a mistake;

Republican leaders who had vainly watched King Charles Albert wreck Italian hopes in the north thronged down to Rome, where there seemed to be a fighting chance for pure Republican principles. One of the most important of them was Garibaldi, who set off south from Ravenna at the head of over 500 Legionaries in red shirts or red fezzes – not, perhaps, a large number, but far above their numerical importance in this war of half-hearted masses of troops, and led by the most brilliant irregular general of his time. Garibaldi was the force – the arm, as it might be – of the new Roman Republic that he saw coming; another man was its mind and soul. Herzen, the Russian refugee, has left a description of him:

> Mazzini got up, and, looking me straight in the face with his piercing eyes, held out both hands in a friendly way. Even in Italy a head so severely classical, so elegant in its gravity, is rarely to be met with. At moments the expression of his face was harshly austere, but it quickly grew soft and serene. An active, concentrated intelligence sparkled in his melancholy eyes; there was infinity of persistence and strength of will in them and in the lines on his brow. All his features showed traces of long years of anxiety, of sleepless nights, of past storms, of powerful passions or rather of one powerful passion, and also some element of fanaticism – perhaps of asceticism.[217]

(But the story of the Roman Republic also is a story of 1849. It too, after a nobler record even than the Hungarians', was murdered by an alien invasion – in this case French.)

Across the Atlantic there was what all foreign observers

presumed to be a victory for freedom. General Lewis Cass, Democrat, was defeated for the Presidency of the United States by General Zachary Taylor, Whig. Those who believed or hoped that this was a conflict between a 'slavocrat' and a liberator were hardly more than a third right. They knew nothing of the complexity of American politics. Certainly, men like Greeley and Abraham Lincoln[218] campaigned for Taylor, and the

Arms of the United States in 1848

man himself was far more likeable than his opponent. But he was a slave-holder, with 300 slaves, and both parties evaded the question in their programmes even though it was in everybody's mind – that is, not the question of liberating the slaves, for that was not considered practical politics, but the question whether the newly conquered lands should be slave or free. The evasiveness of both parties even on this limited question was such that a small group of discontented men put forward Van Buren as a candidate, but they too did not come forward as liberators, calling themselves the 'Free

Soil' party, and concentrating on the grievances of the impoverished whites.[219] They seem, indeed, to have drawn votes mostly from Cass, for their 'treason' was given as the cause of his only receiving 127 electoral votes against Taylor's 163. With Taylor there was returned as Vice-President a man called Millard Fillmore, little-noticed and of little importance. The campaign biography of him printed in the *American Review*[220] is almost discourteous in its listlessness. He was 'born to comparative poverty' and had 'struggled bravely with difficulties', the voters read, and his chief characteristic was 'a thorough attention to duty'. The character of the rough and honest man who was his superior was far more important; those observers were correct who believed that in office he would prove better and more generous than his programme. They may have foreseen that he would in fact prevent the extension of slavery to California. They could not have foreseen that he would die suddenly in office, and his place be taken by the dull and rather mean-minded man whom the needs of party politics had put into the trivial office of Vice-President.

X

December

*

THE cycle of revolutions had begun in France; it was fitting that it should close in France. Many of those who were close to the event did not or would not realize what had happened; but at a little distance from Paris it was clear to everybody that what came this month was the end. Among the false Robespierres, Dantons and Vergniauds there was one imitator of the first revolutionary period who had played his role to complete success – so much so that he now dropped the 'Louis' from his name and just called himself Napoleon Bonaparte.

He owed his success in part to his insignificance, or perhaps rather to a successfully assumed appearance of insignificance. The record of his hopelessly bungled plottings while Louis Philippe was King, and his later failures in February and in June of this year was reinforced by his poor showing when he decided to take a seat in the Assembly, to which he had been again elected in the autumn. His infrequent speeches were so poorly delivered and ineffective that the member who had intended to move that he should not be allowed to stand for President, abandoned the motion. The man was of no possible importance, he said, advancing an argument often used later; it was only the publicity given to him by his opponents that blew him up into a size larger than a frog. His colourlessness, indeed, encouraged some Conservative statesmen to make use of him. MM. Thiers, de Girardin and other half-forgotten politicians who thought themselves and were thought by most observers to be the most skilled of tacticians, took him up as a sort of lay figure which they could easily manipulate afterwards if he became President.[221] They put forward his candidature seriously and ran a campaign for him in the Paris papers. Victor Hugo, the poet, joined with them; he repented it bitterly later. There were four other candidates: General Cavaignac who was in the best position of all, as the presumed saviour of society and the effective head of the state; Ledru-Rollin who could hardly expect to win but would assemble all the votes of the Republican Left; Lamartine who only a few months ago had been the incarnate voice of France, and whom seventeen constituencies had elected as their member; and Raspail, a devoted doctor much loved by the Parisians.

The election took place on a fine winter Sunday, December 10th, and 7,426,252 voters went to the poll. It was seen then that MM. Thiers, de Girardin and the rest could have spared themselves their trouble. The provinces had made their choice already. The figures were:

Napoleon Bonaparte . . .	5,534,520
General E. Cavaignac . . .	1,448,302
A. A. Ledru-Rollin	371,431
Dr. Raspail	36,964
Alphonse de Lamartine . . .	17,914[222]

There were some trifling changes made in the final count. 4,600 votes were given to a general named Changarnier.

The new President attended to take the oath on December 20th in front of the Assembly. He occupied his usual seat in the House, sitting as he always did next to his old teacher, a man called Vieillard; there was still nothing noticeable about him – he was short, narrow-eyed, sallow, and his hair was thinning. He wore a blue suit with a white waistcoat, which hostile

THE YOUNG REPUBLIC OF FRANCE CONTEMPLATING SUICIDE.

observers said made him look like a gymnasium attendant.[223] He clambered up to the platform when his name was called, and faced the President of the Assembly, or Speaker as he would be called in England and America, whose name was Armand Marrast. The confrontation of the two men was something like a confrontation of two principles.

Enough has been said about Bonaparte; he was the prototype of Mussolini; perhaps of Hitler too. Armand

December

Marrast's name has appeared twice in this history, once as a member of the first Republican Government, once as Mayor of Paris during the ridiculous revolt of May 15th. In both those offices and in his present one he was a figure of importance; he is forgotten now – indeed, he was already forgotten in three years' time when he was dying, so much so that those who were asked to subscribe for his coffin had to be reminded who he was. He was a small man from the Pyrenees, dark, lively, a witty conversationalist and writer; not so much handsome as elegant and impeccably dressed. He was the pure Republican – a man for whom the words Liberty, Equality and Fraternity comprised everything that was valuable and honourable in the world, and for whom the idea of the Republic contained something divine; but he did not understand one word of Louis Blanc's *Organization of Labour*. When he was imprisoned with many others in the prison of Ste.-Pelagie during the thirties, he organised and took part in a ceremonial whose ritual seems as strange to us today as the fact that it was allowed. It was called, he recorded, the Evening Prayer. As darkness fell, 'certain of the proletarians' carried a tricolour flag down into the courtyard and formed a circle round it. All the republicans then came down and joined them, and one would sing the *Chant du départ*. Everyone joined in the chorus – 'all those strong male voices, this silence, this comradeship, liberty praised and exalted, the presence of the three colours, the men whose faith blazed out from them – all this made a sort of holy-day for which Hope provided the altar'. The ceremony ended with the *Marseillaise*, the last verse being sung kneeling, eyes to the sky. 'When the hymn was over, the ensign made the round of the audience;

each man kissed the three colours and then stood up.'[224] To this religious republicanism he linked an almost equal enthusiasm for the civilized life – painting, poetry, music, fine prose, fine clothes, fine wines were as much part of the true Republic as free speech and wide tolerance. He despised the vulgarity of the rich bourgeois as much as his political servility. 'We have on our side youth and strength, the artist who creates, the people which works, genius and knowledge – the two starting points of the revolution.' When he returned from exile, he had become editor of the *National*, the most successful daily of its kind, and he had seen his contributors and colleagues take the highest offices in February 1848. They had dropped out, one by one now, and he himself was being weakened by a mysterious unpopularity. His life was too elegant; Blanqui had fixed on him the nickname that never left him: he had called him 'the Marquis of the Republic'. He would give two fingers to de Rothschild, forgiving him his wealth and his barony in order to show that a Republican had no prejudice against a Jew, but the same superbity made him, as President of the Assembly, resume the practice of the giving of official dinners and balls, soon after the days of June were over. They were brilliant and expensive; many guests attended, even Lord Normanby the British Ambassador, with his suave dislike and his freezing wife, but Marrast could never understand why Ledru-Rollin and his followers of the Left sent back their invitation cards, as if they were insults. Paris had always depended on luxury trades; the workers were hungry; surely he was only helping to re-start the clothing, food and furniture trades at their most expensive ends?

Physically also he was weakening. The cholera had

given him a flick of its whip; he could no longer work or write as he once had. His voice had failed him; a few sentences full of his old sarcasm were all that he could usually manage.[225] Today, for the last time, his voice maintained its old strength as he looked steadily at the man before him and required him to swear the oath of loyalty to the Republic. Bonaparte did not look at him, but answered in a clear and firm voice: 'Before God and before man, I swear loyalty to the Constitution of the French Republic.' Marrast, whose face was white and set, proclaimed him 'President of the French Republic from this day until the second Sunday of May, 1852'.

(A little time before that date, when he was very ill, his doctor told him that Bonaparte had destroyed the Republic and made himself Emperor. 'Well, doctor,' said Marrast, pointing upwards with a last smile, 'I am dying, so I can take his oath with me.')

The fine Sunday of the vote was almost the last mild day of the year, and for that everyone soon had reason to be grateful. There had been no touch of winter yet.[226] Cholera had spread relentlessly, throwing out long tentacles or sprays like a poisonous climber or a bind-weed. St. Petersburg to Berlin, Berlin to Hamburg, Hamburg to Edinburgh, Edinburgh to New York and New Orleans, New Orleans up the rivers to Cincinnati – its course has already been traced, and none of the doctors' remedies stopped it. Now it was halted suddenly, by the same force as kills bindweed: frost. The bitter, welcome cold came down again from the north; the disease faltered, shrank, and vanished. But that it was ended few people would have cared to swear; it might well, like bindweed, re-appear as strong as ever with the spring.

Even with that doubt there seems to have been a

revival of cheerfulness. There is almost a primitive happiness in the paragraph which appeared on the front page of the *New York Daily Tribune*:

☞ Reluctant as we are to say anything about the weather, as our readers well know, we are compelled by a sense of justice to notice the present beautiful moonlight evenings. It makes one actually long for night.

However, sentimentality of that or any other kind did not last long with Horace Greeley, the Editor. Almost at once he turned back to his task of reform through denunciation. The New York streets he inspected and found 'indescribably loathsome and disgusting'. President Polk's Message to Congress he described as 'a tissue of sickening self-laudation'.[227] (It certainly was intolerably long; the English *Annual Register* which felt itself compelled to reprint most of it complained of the space that it took; happily ignorant of what was to come, it added that no President in the future was likely to be guilty of such 'inordinate verbosity'.) The paper could praise as well as blame; it commended what could have been a great advance in medicine, in a long study of a new book by Dr. W. Channing, called *Etherization in Childbirth*. It was unusual to give a column on the front page to a book review. But this was the first practical manual for painless labour, and the instruction given in it had the approval of Professor Simpson, the inventor of chloroform; the *Tribune's* examination of it declared it to be safe and demanded its general adoption. Vainly, of course; the clergy at once replied with overwhelming denunciations. 'In sorrow shalt thou bring forth children'; it was so written in the third

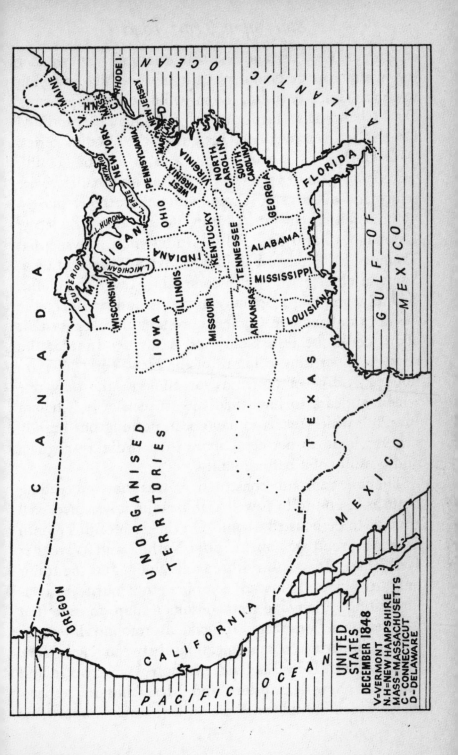

UNITED
STATES
DECEMBER 1848
V = VERMONT
N.H = NEW HAMPSHIRE
MASS = MASSACHUSETTS
C = CONNECTICUT
D = DELAWARE

chapter of Genesis, and the sole question was whether the woman or the doctor was the more wicked in trying to evade God's decision. Even while he was supporting Dr. Channing's medical enlightenment editorially, Greeley's advertising columns puffed the old quackeries. 'Dr. Christie's Galvanic Belt and Magnetic Fluid', priced at $3 and $1 respectively, set up (readers were informed) a Galvanic Circulation in the body and so without fail cured 'Fits, Cramp, Rheumatism, Epilepsy, Lumbago, Paralysis, Palsy, Indigestion, Dyspepsia, Tremors, Stiff Joints, Palpitations, Apoplexy, Neuralgia, Pains in chest or side, Hip complaint, Liver complaint, Kidney complaint, Spinal complaint and Spasms'; the list does not include Cholera, presumably because that claim could be tested only too easily.[228] Indeed, the reckless advertising columns of the New York press are noticeably free of nostrums for cholera; the only one which appears to have had any success was 'Cholera Brandy', which seems to have been nothing but brandy priced about 20 per cent. more than ordinary cognac, and possibly of a better quality.

Though railroad construction was not proceeding quite as fast or quite as well as in Britain, it was successful enough to be boasted about. On the 20th of this month a new railroad was opened, the Nashua and Worcester Rail Road. It was forty-three miles long, and the trains only took two hours to complete the journey. It is interesting, to anyone who consults a map, to note that its opening was expected to make a profound difference to the imperfect communications between New York and northern New England; the towns are two inland places in New Hampshire and Massachusetts respectively which could only have had such importance through extreme capriciousness in early railway development. Exactly a week later a second railway opening was announced and one which, this time, proved in the end to justify the excitement that it caused. The New York and Erie Railroad opened an extension of 126½ miles, from Port Jervis, the point where the states of New York, New Jersey and Pennsylvania touched, up-country to Binghamton, a growing and important centre of Upper New York State. Twenty years later when the Nashua and Worcester was forgotten, this line was a great artery to the West.[229] It had been cut through 'wild and desolate' country, almost uninhabited and reminding the imaginative guests who rode on the inaugural journey of Hungarian mountains or Russian wastes, with long cuttings winding through gloomy glens and open runs on bleak heaths. Nor did the track seem to be very well laid or organized. The locomotive ran off the rails at one point; at another some workmen 'though instructed not to do so by the superintendent' had left on the rails a 'dirt car', whatever that was; the train struck it and injured two Germans.

The courts in Albany, the capital of New York State, affirmed a new principle of law, which was not destined to be upheld. Captain W. Goodwin, one of the generally pretty brutalized class of canal-boat skippers, was prosecuted for beating his wife and his child, a small girl. The facts were proved and he was punished for beating his daughter, because as a child she was undeveloped and unable to defend herself, and also being young could not be expected to have a full understanding of the faults charged against her; he was not punished for beating his wife, though the court did not expound its principles equally fully here.[320]

But the thoughts of men and the columns of the press in the Eastern States (and indeed even in Europe by now) were not occupied with such things but much more by a subject which had been intermittently referred to and speculated over during the year, and which only now was finally proved to be of unequalled importance. This was the gold that Marshall had found in January in California. There had been wild stories throughout the last nine months, but at last they had been authenticated. Paragraphs in Polk's monstrous and meandering monologue to Congress made it official; the London *Morning Chronicle* in its leader[231] quoted from the Government's observer on the spot, Colonel Mason, the two sentences which answered the two questions everyone was asking: 'There is no ground for quarrelling as yet, because there is enough gold to spare for all. No capital is required as the labourer wants nothing but his pick, shovel and tin pan.'

Many read no more than that, and set off on a journey. Many set off on the same journey for other reasons. The year 1848 ended with an immense and unplanned movement of human beings westward – of Europeans to the United States, of both Europeans and Americans to California. The migrants were of two kinds, with two objects – freedom and gold. They also were of two characters, the worst and the best. Though the most learned historian of the Gold Rush, Hubert Bancroft,[232] says that the earliest comers to California in search of gold were 'just and ingenuous', he admits that almost immediately afterwards they were swamped by hordes of the lowest criminals; it was these last who became the typical gold-seekers. The republicans and reformers who came in search of liberty as they realized that tyranny was returning to Europe were the elite of the population, the noblest, most industrious and clearest-headed. The two classes can be typified by Carl Schurz, the defeated German republican who lived to become one of the most honoured of United States senators, and the unnamed immigrant hanged on the last day of the year near Coloma on the American River, who was described as 'vicious; also a horse-thief and probably a murderer'.

Man cannot live by ideals alone; the two categories were not completely separate, and many revolutionaries saw no reason why in the land of liberty they should not also seek for gold. Against many of the names of one-time active Chartists the contemporary historian Gammage notes 'he is believed to have left for the California diggings'. Those that did so found themselves swept up in a fierce current of greed and hysteria in which their previous preoccupations and even their principles could be quickly forgotten. The reality of the prizes offered could not be doubted; not only was there the President's authentication but a tea-caddy full of gold dust was on exhibition at the War Office in Washington, sent there by Colonel Mason for examination. Other samples abounded; one, sent by a soldier to New York, was submitted 'to an optician in Nassau Street' and pronounced pure gold. Californian gold 'exceeds calculation – reminds us of the treasures of Aladdin', decided the *Tribune* and the staider *New York Journal of Commerce* reported, fairly truthfully:

At present the people there are running over the country and picking gold out of the earth here and there just as a thousand groundhogs let loose in a

forest would root up groundnuts. Some get eight to
ten ounces a day, and the least active one or two.
There is one man who has sixty Indians in his pay;
his profits are a dollar a minute.[233]

There were three routes by which Aladdin's Cave
could be reached. The sensiblest and surest way was
round Cape Horn, up to the West coast of South
America, and so in due course to the tiny towns of
Monterey or San Francisco (population: males, 575;
females, 177; children, 60).[234] Rasher, but apparently
quicker, was to take a ship to Chagres on the Panama
isthmus, cross the land by boat and pack-horse, and hope
to find a ship going north from Panama City on the
other side. Rashest of all was to take what seemed
the shortest route and go straight across the prairie from
the eastern States to California.

The first route, the long sea route, was the most
used in 1848, and the most successful always. It had
the odd result that California was more accessible to
other nations than to its nominal owners, the Americans
of the United States. European ships could reach Cape
Horn as soon or sooner than those from Boston or New
Orleans; even Hawaiians, Australians and Chinamen
were more prominent among the earliest arrivals. (The
very first, naturally, were the Oregonians who deserted
the territory Polk had so recently acquired for them,
and the Mexicans who till a year ago had ruled there –
'the whole state of Sonora 'was' on the move'.)[235]
Indeed, the Americans would not have been properly
represented at all, but for two accidents. The first
was that soldiers and sailors were still being sent to
California in the early part of the year, as though the

Mexican war was still being fought, and the second that by a fortunate hazard a sea-mail service had just been inaugurated, served by three paddle-steamers. The first, the *California*, had left New York on October 6th. So little were the rumours credited then that she carried no passengers at all for California. So sudden and violent was the stampede that when she touched at Panama on the way up the West coast she was almost rushed by 'some 1,500 gold-seekers', who had all taken the second route and crossed the Isthmus in the hope of finding on board of her a cabin, a bunk, a seat or even a coil of rope to lie on. They had easily enough found sailing ships or steamships to take them across the Caribbean to Chagres; then they had gone up the river as far as it was navigable in 'bongos or dugouts, poled by naked negroes as lazy and vicious as they were stalwart';[236] then with their luggage they had ascended and descended an old, broken, paved trail across the mountains, to find in Panama a raging cholera which there was no winter chill to stop.

Those who tried the overland route across the Rocky Mountains suffered even more. Soon after crossing the Mississippi they had left all organized life behind them. The new state of Texas claimed large areas in the west, but its possession of them was imaginary; the little Mormon state of Deseret in what is now Utah was off the route, and anyway regarded the migrants as persecutors and enemies. Otherwise the inhabitants were Red Indians; later sentimentalities have disguised the fact that they were savages, and a horrible death was all that could be expected of them. But many more travellers were killed by natural causes – thirst in the deserts, intense heat and bitter cold on the prairie and in the mountains, and hunger. Plain exhaustion was a common cause. One letter, not exceptional in any way, says:[237]

> The great dessert from the sink to Truckee's river was an awfull place. The water at the warm springs in the centre was poisenous to all kinds of stock and the road on the dessert was lined with dead cattle, mules & horses with here and there a wagon, & all kinds of property in large quantities thrown away. . . . The road from and up the Truckee river to the summit of the Serra Navada was bad but the road from the summit to Johnson's settlement is the most *damniabl* road on the face of the earth. You must excuse such an expression but if you only knew of and could have seen the hard labor we have expended on it you would all say so. It was filled with large rocks from the size of a teakettle up to that of a hogshead, over which we were obliged to drive or rather lift the wagons. It is certainly the most miserable gloomy road on earth.

The emigrants made their sufferings worse by the grotesque luggage they brought with them. Greeley's advice to take a rubber tent fitted with a bed, candlestick and candle was relatively sensible; less intelligent was that to bring a special rubber boat to go up and down the Sacramento and San Joaquin Rivers, off which were to be found the most successful diggings. But many brought 'everything a man's wife or a boy's mother could think of – sheet iron stoves, feather beds, pillows, pillowslips, blankets, quilts and comforters . . . trunks full of white shirts and plug hats . . . one man was hauling a great walnut bed-stead'.[238] The same observer who wrote this claimed to have noticed abandoned on the road 'bar-iron and steel, large black-smith's anvils and bellows, crowbars, drills, augers, gold washers, chisels, axes, lead, trunks, spades, ploughs, large grindstones, baking ovens and cooking stoves'.

It was the more pathetic because, in this first year, they would have needed none of those tools. The reports were quite truthful: miners were in fact prising nuggets

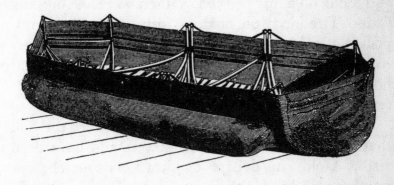

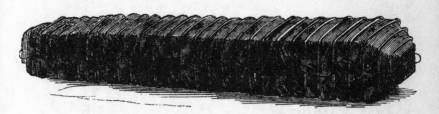

Goodyear's portable india-rubber boat for emigrants to California

of gold out with their knives, and the better equipped were only using some simple washing devices called the rocker and the cradle. By these means they were collecting fabulous amounts. Marshall in his first discovery had collected half a pint of gold without digging at all, in pieces 'up to the size of a bean'. At the camps (or 'bars' as they were called) of Parks, Long and Foster miners using the most ineffective tools made

between $60 and $100 a day. At the place called Spanish
Bar a party of industrious Mormons made ultimately the
fabulous figure of $1,000,000. But they were unusual,
in that they kept their money; most miners lost it or
wasted it. Marshall himself was penniless and wandering, hating his fellow men for some reason and hated by
them; he became a spiritualist and ended up half crazy
and living on a tiny pension. Others were like the famous
Chino Tirador, who made a fortune by discovering a
pocket of gold dust so large that 'with a horn spoon' he
collected so much that it was more than he could carry,
bought some whisky, started a game of monte and by
ten o'clock that night was 'penniless and drunk'.

Nor, for those that held on to them, were the dollars
that they gained worth what they should have been in
1848. Gold, in dollars or dust, became cheap. A
storekeeper's bill for the ingredients of a small lunch for
two in Coloma this month was:

1 box sardines . . .	$16
1 lb. hard bread . . .	$2
1 lb. butter	$6
½ lb. cheese	$3
2 bottles ale	$16
	$43

The governor, Colonel Mason, was both shocked and
incommoded by having to pay half an ounce of gold for a
Seidlitz Powder.

That was only one of his anxieties. He was not even
sure that he had the right to call himself governor. He
was only the military commander; peace had been
proclaimed in this area on August 7th, but he could get

from Washington neither authorization to act as governor
himself nor instructions on setting up a government. He
lacked even power to enforce his authority; his soldiers
left him as fast as they dared to go to the diggings. It
was impossible to prevent desertions, or to apprehend
deserters; 'no officer can now live in California on his
pay, money has so little value', he reported vainly to
headquarters. Indeed, not only his barracks but whole
towns seem to empty themselves as he watched; Monterey was so deserted that at one time he had to cook his
own dinner; 'three-quarters' of the men had left San
Francisco; there were reported to be 'no males in
Sonoma, San José and Santa Cruz'.[239] The ship
California could not return to New York because the
moment she docked all her crew deserted and went to
the diggings. Sailors were signing on in the eastern ports
to go to California at a wage of $1 a month; but none
would take the journey back at any price at all.[240]

If there had been an observer in England or America
on the last day of 1848, sitting at a desk in a Foreign
Office, in the news-room of a daily paper, or some other
place where he could have had all or nearly all the
information that we have today, he might easily have
given a melancholy verdict on the year that was passing.
In America there was a senseless rush westward moti-
vated by mere greed, and it did not need much gift of
prophecy to foresee the next few years of degradation
and violence which Californian historians try to forget or
to glamorize. In Europe there was a steady destruction of
liberty, and the restoration of Kings and Emperors who
were now dishonoured as well as despotic. True, there
were still two lights burning. Mazzini in Italy was
making of the Roman Republic a sort of secular City of

God, controlled and disciplined by his own shining
virtue; but anyone could guess that it would be short
lived. Kossuth's Hungarian Republic was less whitely
radiant and more many-coloured, a story written by
Walter Scott rather than by St. Francis; and round it
too were gathering the shadows of dark armies. The
verdict could easily be the confident one that Lord
Normanby was writing in his diaries – that the undisciplined year had left 'almost every individual less
happy, every country less prosperous, every people not
only less free but less hopeful of freedom hereafter'.[241]
But if this observer had been not only uniquely well-
informed but also preternaturally acute in mind, he
might have realized that the legs of the thrones on to
which the monarchs climbed back were shaky. They
had been broken once, and imperfectly repaired. Within the next half century every one of the restored dynast-
ies was to find it prudent to accept two-thirds or more
of the reforms that they now so gleefully tore up.
Parliaments, a free judiciary, personal liberty, freedom
of the press, democratic control of the purse and even of
the executive, – all of these were to become more or less
standard in all the countries which the flame of 1848 had
scorched; it was to be of some considerable importance
for the future unhappiness of their people that Spain and
Russia had not been touched by it. If his sight had been
sharp enough to reach as far as 1918, he would have
noticed with some pleasure that only those families
would keep their thrones who had kept their promises
to their peoples in 1848 – the Dutch, the Dane and the
Piedmontese. The multitudinous others would be in
exile with no hope of return.

In fact, of course, no such visions would have been

likely to occur to him. He would have turned for
consolation to the thoughts natural to English-speakers
around Christmas. Certainly, there was crime and
misery still; on Christmas Eve itself a criminal described
as 'alias the Saint' was brought up at Lambeth – his
real name, modern thriller-readers may care to know,
was James Ludlan and he had stolen £375 from public
houses. But just as Dickens' Fagins and Squeerses were
true portraits, so too were the cheerfuller characters –
the great turkey, which was so fat 'he never could have
stood upon his legs' was as real as Scrooge for one part
of the year at least. Over Christmas and the New
Year there was always a rush of real charity, a flood of
generosity and good nature which in that smaller society
did for a short time undo or mitigate the miseries of
poverty or unemployment. There was a great outpour-
ing of gross good things, greatly needed and for once
available to all or nearly all. It is impossible, even today,
not to feel some coarse and ordinary glee when reading
the advertisement columns of the papers at this time.
Sucking-pigs, barrels of oysters, brawn, poultry, game,
sausages – or, if you are more particular, will you have
from Morel's *fois gras* in crust, game *pâtés*, Spanish and
Westphalia hams, *jambonneaux de Strasbourg*, *fromage de
cochon*, Pomeranian geese, Perigord truffles, Lyons and
Bologna sausages, *marrons du luc*, anchovies, tunny,
Severn smoked salmon, boars' heads, and Yorkshire
pies of all kinds? Or, from Pussell's, Christmas Cakes
of all qualities and sizes from 1s. upwards? Or Honduras
Turtle soup at 7s. 6d. the quart? Will you accept, or
give to someone else, 12 lb. of coffee roasted in silver
cylinders and packed in six magnums for £1? Perhaps
you prefer tea? Black tea: the common Congou is

2s. 10d. to 3s. a pound, the Ouloong, which costs 24 to 45 taels in China, is 3s. 8d. and 4s. 8d. Green tea is dearer: the Young Hyson, costing 36 to 54 taels, is 4s. 0½d. to 5s. 2d. and 'Gunpowder' runs as high as 5s. 10d. But it would be a poor heart that rejoiced on tea; there is better drink within the reach of all. Port is half a crown a bottle, so is sherry – 3s. 6d. for the very best quality – marsala 2s. and Cape wines of the same character 1s. 6d. Spirits? Whisky, 18s.; rum, 12s.; Gin, 8s. to 12s.; – not per bottle, but per gallon. There is also a thing called British Brown Brandy at 18s. a gallon, but if you are wise you will leave that alone. It is distilled from potatoes and coloured by a dark, caramel-like mixture whose composition is a secret and which is supposed to make it taste like cognac. It does not; it scarcely conceals the rawness of the alcohol. Better to pay 6s. more and buy the genuine article. If that is beyond your purse, you may care to note that Bass's October brew of East India Pale Ale is 'just now arriving from Burton-on-Trent, in fine condition'.

These excellent things were by no means reserved for the rich, at least at this period of the year. The *Observer*, in common with other papers, felt that its readers could not sit down comfortably to their Christmas dinners if they felt that others less fortunate were starving. It investigated, therefore, what the most miserable of all would be offered on that day, the inhabitants of the work-houses. There were 80,000 dinners of which it got details. Nearly all were hot roast beef dinners; the amount served to each person was ½ lb. of meat or 1 lb., 'without bone'. Those that did not have roast beef had a similar amount of roast pork, stuffed with sage and onions; some lucky ones had the choice. There was of course also 1 lb. each of potatoes, or more '*ad lib*.'; the main dish was invariably followed by plum pudding – again 1 lb. per head, with trimmings, which it is safe to assume included rum or brandy sauce. There were tea, sugar and cakes in varying quantities and porter in an unvarying quantity – 1 pint, except in one workhouse whose rash guardians placed no limit on it.

The year must have ended for most people in much the same way; thoughts and actions at Christmas and the New Year fall, and fell then, much into the same pattern. Alexis Soyer for example; he had seen to it that his free kitchen at Spitalfields in the East End had given larger meals than usual over the season; he had visited it in the late afternoon to see that all was well and returned to his kingdom in the Reform Club to supervise the cooking of the dinner for the members. The last meal of the year was probably a remarkable one, but the menu has not been preserved. Just before the stroke of midnight, he went outside, the only club servant of sufficiently assured position to stand on the steps with the rich and distinguished who were going to salute the New Year. He had his hat in his hand – perhaps his Idroto-bolic Hat – and stood, I suppose as beamingly contented as ever, under the full moon as the bells of Westminster Abbey broke the silence in a great waterfall of sound.

References

1. General Report on the Sanitary Condition of the Labouring Population, 1842, 14, 16, 24, 33, 111, 125, 131, 253.
2. *Early Victorian England*, ed. G. M. Young, i., 184.
3. *Annual Register*. Chronicle, January 1st.
4. *Ibid.*, 1848, 'Chronicle', January, 31st.
5. Young, *op. cit.*, 87-8.
6. S. and B. Webb, *English Poor Law History*, Part II, vol. i, 186 *sqq.*
7. Young, *op. cit.*, i, 46.
8. J. L. and B. Hammond, *The Age of the Chartists*, 351.
9. Thomas Cooper, *The Life of Thomas Cooper*, 311.
10. R. W. Emerson, *English Traits*, 107, 115 (World's Classics edition).
11. Emerson, *op. cit.*, 131, 132, 135.
12. *Ibid.*, 124, 171, 176.
13. Young, *op. cit.*, i, 124.
14. *Morning Chronicle*, advertisement columns, January to March.
15. *The Red Republican.*
16. *Message to Congress.*
17. R. G. Cleland, *From Wilderness to Empire*, 234, 239.
18. Harvey O'Connor, *The Astors*, 24, 39, 50, 58, 83, 97.
19. O'Connor, *op. cit.*, 59, 50.
20. *Punch*, 1848, vol. ii, 205.
21. *Annual Register*, 1848, ii, 20.
22. *Ibid.*, 1848, ii, 333-363.
23. Justin McCarthy, *History of Our Own Times*, ii, 22.
24. G. E. Maurice, *Revolutions of 1848 and 1849*, 214.
25. Maurice. *op. cit.*, 240.
26. K. Marx and F. Engels, *Revolution and Counter Revolution*, 63.
27. *Ibid.*, 64.
28. E. O. S., *Hungary and Its Revolutions*, 1854, 162.

29. J. G. Legge, *Rhyme and Revolution in Germany*, 168.

30. Lord Normanby, *A Year of Revolution*, i, 46 *sqq*. P. Audebrand *Mémoires d'un Passant*, 214.

31. *Annual Register*, 1848, ii, 216, 224.

32. G. M. Theal, *History of South Africa, 1834-1854*, ii, 308 *sqq*.

33. Theal, *op. cit.*, ii, 314.

34. *Ibid.*, ii, 320, 329, 353, 360, 426.

35. Norman Gash, *Politics in the Age of Peel*, 397 *sqq*.

36. *Ibid.*, 439.

37. *Annual Register*, 1848, 'Chronicle', 253.

38. Justin McCarthy, *History of Our Own Times*, i, 388.

39. Hesketh Pearson, *'Dizzy'*, 81.

40. *Ibid.*, 27 *sqq*., 86.

41. Spencer Walpole, *Life of Lord John Russell*, ii, 24.

42. *Annual Register*, 1848, i, 38 *sqq*.

43. Select Committee on the Slave Trade (House of Lords), published 1849, evidence of *Winniett*.

44. *Ibid.*, *Matson*; W. L. Mathieson, *Britain and the Slave Trade*, 63, 141.

45. Chris Lloyd, *The Navy and the Slave Trade*, 45, 47.

46. *Ibid.*, 58.

47. W. L. Mathison, *op. cit.*, 67; *Encyclopaedia Britannica*, 14th ed, *s.v.* 'Cass, Lewis'.

48. Lords' Committee, *Staveley, Howdin, Herring*.

49. *Ibid.*, *Matson*.

50. *Ibid.*, *Hesketh*.

51. *Ibid.*, 248.

52. Lloyd, *op. cit.*, 29.

53. T. Canot, *Memoirs of An African Slave Trader*, 316, in Lloyd, *op. cit.*

54. *Op. cit.*, 240.

55. Lloyd, *op. cit.*, 17.

56. *Ibid.*, 130.

57. Lords' Committee, *Staveley*.

58. *Morning Chronicle*, February 16th, *sqq*.

59. Text in *State Trials*, 1848.

60. Lloyd, *op. cit.*, 94 *sq*.

References

61. *Ibid.*, 96.

62. *Ibid.*, 139.

63. Garnier Pagès, *Histoire de la Revolution de 1848*, i, 228-31.

64. P. de la Gorce, *Histoire de la 2nd Republique*, i, Bk. 2; A Crémieux, *La Revolution de Février*, *passim*; Blanc, *Histoire de la Revolution de 1848*, i. 47.

65. P. Audebrand, *Nos Revolutionnaires*, 119; N. W. Senior, *Conversations with M. Thiers*, etc., 15-26 for another account.

66. Lord Normanby, *A Year of Revolution*, 182; K. Gavin, *Louis Philippe*, 144; *Annual Register*, 'Chronicle', November 17th.

67. R. Postgate, *Revolution from 1789 to 1906*, 186-200; A. Crémieux, *La Revolution de Février*, 409 *sqq*.

68. Normanby, *op. cit.*, 140, 142, 212

69. *Annual Register*, 'Chronicles', February 29th.

70. Hans Blum, *Die Deutsche Revolution*, 80, 135, 186, 196; J. G. Legge, *Rhyme and Revolution in Germany*, 235-59; Postgate, *op. cit.*, 239-63.

71. Legge, *op. cit.*, 303.

72. *Ibid.*, 240 *sqq.*; C. E. Maurice, *op. cit.*, 240 *sqq*.

73. G. M. Trevelyan, *Manin*, ch. iv.

74. *Ibid.*, ch. vi.

75. G. M. Trevelyan, *Garibaldi's Defence of Rome*, 65.

76. Postgate, *op. cit.*, 193 *sqq.*; A. de Lamartine, *Revolution of 1848*, Bk. ix. *passim.*; J. F. Jeanjean, *Armand Barbès*, i. 137 *sqq*.

77. Postgate, *op. cit.*, 198-206; E. Thomas, *Histoire des Ateliers Nationaux*, 35-152; F. Dreyfus *L'Assistance sous la 2me Republique*, 46-50; L. Blanc, *La Revolution au Luxembourg*, 45.

78. L. de la Hodde, *Histoire des Sociéties Secrètes*, 502; Philibert Audebrand, *Memoires d'un passant*, 222 *sqq*.

79. *Memoirs of Citizen Caussidière*, ii, 76.

80. Emerson, *op. cit.*, 151

81. R. G. Gammage, *History of Chartism*, 313-22.

82. See for all this R. S. Lambert, *The Cobbett of the West*; *Morning Chronicle*, March 29th.

83. Lambert, *op. cit.*, 35.

84. Legge, *op. cit.*, 354.

85. *Ibid.*, 360.

86. Gammage, *History of Chartism*, 321; J. Saville, *Ernest Jones*, 99.

87. Gammage, *op. cit.*, 324; E. Dolléans, *Le Chartisme*, ii, 415 *sqq.*

88. Julius West, *History of the Chartist Movement*, 245.

89. George Woodcock, *A Hundred Years of Revolution*, 249.

90. Lord Dalmeny, *An Address to the Middle Classes on the Subject of Gymnastic Exercises.*

91. H. C. F. Bell, *Palmerston*, i. 409.

92. W. Holman Hunt, *Pre-Raphaelitism*, i, 101.

93. *Annual Register*, 1848, 'Chronicle', 52.

94. Justin McCarthy, *History of our Own Times*, ii, ch. i.

95. *Morning Chronicle*, April 11th to 15th.

96. Spencer Walpole, *Life of Lord John Russell*, ii, 69.

97. McCarthy, *op. cit.*, ii, 12.

98. *Annual Register*, 1848, i, p. 248.

99. *Fonetic Jurnal*, April, September.

100. Thomas Frost, *Forty Years' Recollections*, 54.

101. *Ibid.*, 40 *sqq.*

102. G. D. H. Cole and R. Postgate, *The Common People, 1746-1946*, 321 *sqq.*

103. *Illustrated News, Lloyd's Weekly Newspaper*, etc., April 30th *sqq.*

104. Soyer records at Reform Club. *Morning Chronicle*, May 15th.

105. R. and S. Redgrave, *A Century of British Painters.*

106. R. H. Wilenski, *English Painting*, 220.

107. May 6th and 13th. See also Groves's *Dictionary of R.A. Exhibitors*, 68.

108. F. G. Stephens, *Sir Edwin Landseer*, 91; Cook's *Handbook to Tate Gallery* (1912), 146.

109. Stephens, 83, 92.

110. W. P. Frith, *Autobiography*, i. 60.

111. *Ibid.*, i, 178, 271; iii, 217.

112. W. Holman Hunt, *Pre-Raphaelitism and the P.R.B.*, i, 166.

113. Groves, *op. cit.*, 30; *Athenaeum*, May 20th.

114. Hunt, i, 82.

115. *Ibid.*, i, 159.

References

116. *Ibid.*, i, 107.

117. R. H. Wilenski, *English Painting*, 220.

118. Hunt, i, 135.

119. F. Bickley, *Pre-Raphaelite Comedy*, 11.

120. C. E. Maurice, *op. cit.*, 353.

121. Legge, *op. cit.*, 534. The date of this is May of next year, when there was a recrudescence of revolt.

122. Robert von Mohl, *Lebenserinnerungen* ii and Laube *Das erste Deutsche Parlament* i, in Legge, *op. cit.*, 368 *sqq.*

123. Maurice Dommanget *Un Drame en '48*, 20, 53, 116; 'Daniel Stern' (Countess d'Agoult), *Histoire de la Revolution de 1848*, iii, 1-35; J. F. Jeanjean, *Armand Barbès*, i, 150 *sqq.*; A. Zevaes, *A. Blanqui*, 50-69; G. Geffroy, *L'Enfermé*, 147-79.

124. H. Castille, *Histoire de la 2me. Republique*, ii, 388 *sqq*; G. Bouniols, *Histoire de la Revolution de 1848*, 159-63; P. de la Gorce, *op. cit.*, i, 254 *sqq.*; *Memoires d'Odilon Barrot*, ii, 188-99; S. Wasserman, *Les Clubs de Barbès et de Blanqui*, 173 *sqq.*

125. Caussidière, *op. cit.*, ii, 139-200; Stern, *op. cit.*, iii, 36-72; de la Gorce, *op. cit.*, i, 257-69.

126. Cf. Curzio Malaparte *Technique du coup d'état*; R. Postgate, *How to make a Revolution.*

127. T. Frost, *Secret Societies*, ii, 204, 215.

128. *Annual Register*, 'Chronicle', 73. *Cf.* Gammage, *op. cit.*, 356.

129. H. C. F. Bell, *Palmerston*, i, 413 *sqq.*

130. *Morning Chronicle*, May 15th.

131. *Early Victorian England*, i, 25.

132. Chart in G. D. H. Cole and R. Postgate, *The Common People, 1746-1946.*

133. Maurice, *op. cit.*, 321 *sqq.*

134. T. Frost, *Recollections of 40 years*, 152 *sqq.*; *Punch*, 1848, 264.

135. R. G. Gammage, *op. cit.*, 353.

136. Charles Schmidt, *Journées de Juin 1848*, 53.

137. R. Pimienta, *Propagande Bonapartiste en 1848*, 36-41.

138. *Ibid.*, 53.

139. A. Ferrère, *Revelations sur la propagande Napoleonnienne*, 74.

140. E. Thomas, *Histoire des Ateliers Nationaux*, 142; *Rapport de la Commission d'Enquete*, i. 352, *sqq.*

141. *Ibid.*, 271, 343.

142. Schmidt, *op. cit.*, 36.

143. Ch. Schmidt, *Les Journees de Juin 1848*, 37; R. Postgate, *Out of the Past*, 107 *sqq.*; R. Postgate, *Revolution from 1789 to 1906*, 211 gives the text of Pujol's pamphlet; M. Wyman, *School Discipline*.

144. See for what follows Schmidt, *op. cit.*, 40 *sqq.*; Louis Menard, *Prologue d'une Revolution*.

145. Normanby, *op. cit.*, ii, 315 *sqq.*; cf. V. Pierre, *Histoire de la Republique de 1848*, 376.

146. Normanby, ii, 84; H. Castille, *op. cit.*, iii, 213 *sqq.*; Menard, *op cit.*, 260.

147. Schmidt, *op. cit.*, 110

148. *Ibid.*, 122. Cf. G. Renard, *Histoire Socialiste*, ix, 82.

149. Menard, *op. cit.*, 275.

150. See Sir L. B. Namier, 'The Revolution of the Intellectuals', *Proceedings of the British Academy*, xxx, 161 *sqq.*

151. R. Postgate, *Revolution*, 273-4.

152. *Bella gerant alii; tu, felix Austria, nube.*
      Nam, quae Mars aliis, dat tibi regna Venus.

153. *Annual Register*, 1848, 'Chronicle', July.

154. *New York Daily Tribune*, April 4th.

155. *Lloyd's Weekly News*, August 6th; see also *Encyclopaedia Britannica*, 14th edn., *s.v.* 'Persia'.

156. *Annual Register*, 1848, 'History', 429 *sqq.*: R. S. Rait, *Life of Lord Gough*, ii, 121 *sqq.*

157. G. M. Theal, *History of South Africa 1834-54*, ii, 430 onwards.

158. *New York Daily Tribune*, August 18th and 19th.

159. *Annual Register*, 1848, 'Chronicle', August.

160. In the *Daily Tribune* throughout the autumn.

161. *New York Tribune*, November 25th.

162. Advertisement columns of *Daily Tribune* and other papers throughout August.

163. *Ibid.*

164. *Troy Post*, August 8th.

165. *Annual Register*, 1848, 'Chronicle', 90.
166. *Buffalo Com. Adv.* August 15th.
167. (Washington) *National Intelligencer*, August 17th.
168. *N.A. Review*, issues of last two quarters of 1848.
169. *National Intelligencer*, August 1st.
170. *Ibid.*
171. *Daily Tribune*, August 9th.
172. *Lloyd's Weekly Newspaper*, August 27th.
173. *Athenaeum*, p. 272.
174. G. M. Young, *op. cit.*, ii, 295.
175. J. H. Clapham, *Economic History of Modern Britain*, i, 391, 396.
176. S. Smiles, *Lives of the Engineers*, iii, 321.
177. Quoted in Clapham, *op. cit.*, i, 412.
178. D. L. Murray, *Disraeli*; H. Pearson, '*Dizzy*', 123; *Annual Register*, 1848, 'Deaths', September.
179. T. Frost, *Secret Societies*, ii, 285.
180. *Northern Star*, June 10th and July 1st.
181. T. Frost, *Forty Years' Recollections*, 149.
182. *State Trials*, vol. vii, Dowling.
183. *Ibid.; Lloyd's Weekly*, August 28th.
184. Frost. *Forty Years' Recollections*, 167; *Annual Register*, 1848, 'Chronicle'.
185. T. Frost, *Forty Years' Recollections*, 164.
186. *Neue Rheinisches Zeitung*, quoted in Maurice, *op. cit.*
187. Maurice, *op. cit.*, 447; J. C. Kastner, *Hungarian Struggle*, 246.
188. H. C. F. Bell, *Lord Palmerston*, i, 44.
189. Leonard Rogers, *Cholera*, 88 *sqq.*; Board of Health instructions in *Annual Register*, 1848, 'Chronicle', 69.
190. *Athenaeum*, November 18th.
191. *Lloyd's Weekly*, August 6th.
192. *Athenaeum*, October 14th.
193. Rogers, *Cholera*, 8.
194. *Ibid.*, 14 *sqq.*
195. *New York Daily Tribune*, August 18th.
196. *National Intelligencer*, November 14th.
197. *New York Tribune* throughout December.

198. *Athenaeum*, October 14th.

199. Rogers, *Cholera*, 14 *sqq.*

200. *Athenaeum*, October 14th.

201. H. D. Traill, *Life of Sir J. Franklin*, 100 *sqq.*

202. Frances J. Woodward, *Portrait of Jane* (Lady Franklin), 245.

203. A. H. Markham, *Life of Sir J. Franklin*, 201.

204. *Athenaeum* October 7th. Cf. *Proceedings* of the British Association, 1848.

205. Woodward, *op. cit.*, 259.

206. *Ibid.*, 258.

207. Traill, *op. cit.*, 386.

208. Markham, *op. cit.*, 224.

209. *Ibid.*; cf. Traill, *op. cit.*, 359 *sqq.*

210. *Ibid.*, 376.

211. *Illustrated London News*, October 28th.

212. Cf. L. Huxley, *Life and Letters of T. H. Huxley*, vol. ii, *passim*.

213. E.g., in *Athenaeum*, October 21st, November 4th, December 2nd, December 4th.

214. R. S. Rait, *Life of Lord Gough*, ii, *passim*.

215. R. G. Gammage, *op. cit.*, 366-7.

216. G. M. Trevelyan, *Garibaldi's Defence of Rome*, 81, 85-7.

217. Geo. Woodcock, *A Hundred Years of Revolution*, 241.

218. R. Hofstadter, *American Political Tradition*, 98.

219. W. E. Binkley, *American Political Parties*, 178.

220. Reprinted in Washington *National Intelligencer*, October 10th.

221. N. W. Senior, *Conversations with M. Thiers*, i, 32-35.

222. G. Bouniols, *Histoire de la Revolution de 1848*, 425; Daniel Stern, *Histoire de la Revolution de 1848*, iii, 344. Cf. Lamartine, *Tribune*, ii, 377.

223. P. Audebrand, *Nos Revolutionnaires*, 113.

224. *Ibid.*, 83, quoting Marrast himself.

225. *Ibid.*, 104 *sqq.*

226. *Punch*, 1848, ii, 272.

227. *Daily Tribune*, December 6th, *sqq.*

228. *Ibid.*, December 12th.

229. *Ibid.*, December 23th and 30th; Appleton's Railway Map of the U.S.A., 1866.

230. *Albany Evening Journal*, December 6th *sqq.*

231. *Morning Chronicle*, December 30th.

232. H. H. Bancroft, *History of the Pacific States*, xviii, 83.

233. *Ibid.*, 115; *Daily Tribune*, November 30th, December 12th; *National Intelligencer*, December 12th.

234. *Ibid.*, August 17th.

235. Bancroft, 111-13.

236. Ibid., 129-30.

237. *California Letters of L. Fairchild*, 35, 36.

238. A. B. Hubbert, quoted in Cleland, *From Wilderness to Empire*, 245.

239. Bancroft, *op. cit.*, 64; *National Intelligencer*, December 12th.

240. *Ibid.*, December 14th.

241. *A Year of Revolution*, i, xiii.

Index

*

281

Index